They Also
Sing
His Praises

They Also Sing His Praises

Margaret Clarkson

Illustrated by Jim Howard

ZONDERVAN
PUBLISHING HOUSE

OF THE ZONDERVAN CORPORATION
GRAND RAPIDS, MICHIGAN 49506

"Yellowthroat," © 1974 by *Christianity Today*. Used by permission.

"Pond Lily," used by kind permission of *Eternity* magazine.

THEY ALSO SING HIS PRAISES
Copyright © 1975 by The Zondervan Corporation
Grand Rapids, Michigan

Library of Congress Cataloging in Publication Data

Clarkson, Edith Margaret, 1915-
    They also sing his praises.

    Published in 1975 under title: Conversations with a barred
owl.
    "New large print ed."
    1. Bird watching. 2. Birds.   3. Large type books.
I. Title.
    [QL677.5.C55   1978]   598.2'073   78-15461
ISBN 0-310-22457-8

Printed in the United States of America

Contents

Foreword

The name of Margaret Clarkson is well-known to many as an accomplished author and hymn writer. It was already known to me, and our paths had crossed briefly on a couple of occasions. But not until I was invited as a fellow bird watcher to contribute a foreword to her latest book did I have the pleasure of meeting her properly. This was at a Christian Leadership Seminar held at York University, Toronto. No sooner was this over than we snatched a few moments to watch migrating warblers in a coppice on the campus. Then the following day I sat with her on the patio of her suburban home, looking out over the ravine she mentions several times in her book and enjoying the red-winged blackbirds which came to her feeder and the stately pheasants strutting by.

So it is a pleasure to write this commendation of a new book by a new friend. We share Jesus Christ, and we also share what Margaret calls "the fraternity of the field glass." Then we have another link. One of her favorite birds is the pileated woodpecker. Indeed, originally this book was to have been called "Someday I'll See a Pileated Woodpecker." This arrested my attention when I read it because within a month or so I expected to be in Northern Michigan and hoped to fulfill a longstanding ambition to see this magnificent creature myself.

It is remarkable that Margaret Clarkson, who has been a bird watcher for only five years, should have accumulated so much bird lore and field experience. She is keenly observant of both sights and sounds, and in prose and poetry alike she uses the artistry of words to record her vivid impressions. Her sense of wonder comes through, also, as she testifies to this new dimension to her life. And her wonder leads to worship, as on that "holy morning" when she held a tiny ruby-throated hummingbird in her hand.

At the end of most chapters she draws an analogy with some aspect of our Christian faith or life and looks through bird-watching to the God of creation behind it all. For this the best of precedents was set by One whose parables were full of allusions to nature.

At the same time, her sense of humor saves her from an excess of piety. How I would love to have eavesdropped on her conversations with loons and owls!

I hope this delightful book will encourage others to take up bird-watching, and I pray that its author will long continue to read spiritual truths in God's creation and give us her insights in writing.

— JOHN STOTT
Rector Emeritus
All Soul's, Langham Place
London, England

Preface

In this little book I offer a group of short sketches about bird life and some of the joys and wonders I have experienced as a bird watcher.

Corollaries between such observations and Christian truth spring readily and with validity to my pen, for their impact on my own life has been both real and powerful. I share these in the hope that others may gain some insights from reading them and perhaps learn to study nature and nature's God for themselves in happy, profitable juxtaposition.

All of life is one, springing from the boundless, creative life of God. I venture to say that there is no natural phenomenon from which we may not learn something enriching about ourselves and our God and the Creator-creature relationship we share. Certainly there is much to be learned spiritually from a study of ornithology.

Where such lessons have been spontaneously real to me, I have not hesitated to write of them. Call it my territorial singing, if you will; I have something to declare that I feel I must say. But I have no desire to manufacture analogy where no natural one has presented itself to me. Hence there are points in these pages where I assert my right to sing just for the sheer joy of living, and I write of some more or less inconsequential happenings. I may not have seen a dramatic portrayal of some spiritual law in any of these sketches, but through all I have experienced a profound sense of wonder, awe, and joy in the God of my salvation. Through them I have worshiped God more truly, and that is reason enough to include them here. I pass this "confession" on in the hope that it may help someone else to do the same.

They Also Sing His Praises

Expectation

This glowing dawn
    all nature stands on tiptoe
        waiting
            drenched with wonder.

Soft air breathes
    mists rise
        waters ripple
            petals stir
                grasses nod
                    leaves sigh.

Birds loose shining shafts of song.

High in the blue
    bright wings drift
        hover and dart.

By fragrant brier
    furred bodies freeze
        nostrils twitch
            whiskers quiver and stiffen
sharp eyes glance
    sure paws flash.

Shimmering insects flit and fall.

        On dewy thorn
            the patient spider weaves
            her jeweled web.

barn swallows

In weedy depths
    of still green waters
        shadowy forms gleam
            silently gliding.
Breezes freshen
    the morning quickens.
Washed in new gold
    all nature waits on tiptoe
        watching
            wordlessly questing,
Is this the day?
    Will it be soon,
The hour of earth's redemption,
    Life's return?

Yellowthroat

I was eighteen that summer and working as companion-housekeeper for a retired school-teacher at her cottage on an island six miles out from the shores of northern Georgian Bay.

She was quite interested in nature and fairly well-versed in its lore. She had a habit, however, of referring to birds and other wild things as if I knew all about them, which was far from the case. City-bred and never having been privileged to enjoy wilderness vacations, although I was fascinated and thrilled by the beauty and wonder around me, I knew almost nothing about it. How grateful I would have been if she had taught me!

The one thing that stands out in my mind from that long-ago, golden summer is that I learned the call of the Maryland yellowthroat. "Witchety, witchety, witchety," my companion would exult every so often, "there's the Maryland yellow-throat!" It never seemed to occur to her, however, to take me to the thickets where the tiny, sprightly elves lived close to the water's edge and show me a yellowthroat or to give me any concrete information about them. I had no idea as to the origin of the witchety little song that rang out so often on that northern island, nor was I aware of the wonders of its nesting habits or the migratory flights that carried the tiny atom of mortality from its breeding grounds in northern Canada, where it is found as far north as the Yukon Territory and Newfoundland, to its winter home in the Caribbean and back again every year. How easily my interest could have been aroused! Yet my employer never thought of really sharing her knowledge of bird life with me.

Nearly thirty-five years were to pass before I caught my first glimpse of that elfin warbler with his brilliant yellow throat and saucy black mask flitting busily and restlessly about in a low thicket at the edge of a stream; and then someone showed him to me. I was utterly captivated. From that moment I took up bird watching as a serious hobby, and life assumed a new and profoundly mean- ingful dimension.

But, oh, the wasted years! Life is too short to wait so long before discovering the rich rewards such a study can bring — joys that were around me all those years, but unrecognized, unheeded. Why didn't someone introduce me to the warbler in that long-ago summer instead of just referring casually to its song?

Yet all too often is not this how we Christians communicate Jesus Christ to our friends? We speak of Him in passing; we acknowledge His presence; but do we actually introduce Him to others? "Show us the Father," said Philip, "and that will be enough for us." Do our lives show Jesus Christ in all His winsome beauty to those around us?

"Behold the Lamb of God!" exclaimed John the Identifier, pointing out the Lord Jesus to two of his own followers. And the two disciples heard him and followed Jesus.

Are others compelled to look at Jesus Christ because of what they see of Him in our lives?

yellowthroat

16

Vireo

I had been watching a red-eyed vireo build her nest about seven feet up in a young maple close to my home. The skillful little weaver worked busily, fashioning an exquisite cup of bits of birch bark, paper from old wasps' nests, leaves, lichens, mosses, and plant fibers. These she bound together with spiders' webs and slung to hang between two supple twigs. When she had lined it with grasses, rootlets, and pine needles, she laid her incredibly tiny eggs — dull white, speckled near the larger end with brownish-red spots.

I watched her daily for nearly two weeks while she incubated, apparently with no help of any kind from her mate. There she sat, patient in wind, sun, and rain, swaying in the breeze, constantly pressing her gentle breast close to her treasures, keeping them safe, warm, and dry. She left the nest only on rare occasions, and then very briefly. During one such interval I found that she was brooding four eggs. The fact that one was somewhat larger than the others did not strike me as significant at the time.

One morning I found that she was absent, and one chick was blindly lifting a gaping bill for food. By evening three downy heads on very wobbly necks were lifted beside his in open-mouthed, mute appeal.

From then on it was easy to see the nestlings, for the mother was absent quite often, searching for food for her famished brood. Father vireo, singing his cheery "question and answer" song from the soaring treetops overhead, seemed to take no part in the proceedings.

It soon became evident that the first-born chick was larger than the other three, more demanding and aggressive. His appearance differed somewhat as well; if anything, he was uglier than the others. But it was not until the fourth day after

17

hatching that the sad truth dawned upon me.

Inspecting the nest that morning, I watched the mother fly off to hunt the endless supply of insects. Tipping the branch slightly to get a better view, I looked into the nest and was struck with horror. The three small nestlings were gone, and the whole space was taken up by the larger one, who had grown to quite astonishing proportions and now filled the nest, great gullet gaping. Three tiny, naked bodies lay on the ground below, dead.

The reason was obvious. A cowbird, a parasitic bird that builds no nest of her own but lays her eggs in the nests of small songbirds, was responsible for the tragedy. Her egg, larger than the others, had hatched first. Her demanding baby had appropriated the greater part of the food brought by the mother. A larger species, it had grown more rapidly and was stronger than the little ones. When the nest had become crowded, it had pushed the tiny vireos to their death. Such is the nature of the cowbird.

Strange to say, the mother vireo continued to feed and raise this ugly chick, driving herself almost beyond endurance in her efforts to satisfy its enormous appetite; yet it had robbed her of her whole family. Poor, gentle little bird, whose instinct to nurture is so great that unwittingly she warms and feeds the source of her own destruction!

"Give no place to the devil," the Scriptures teach us; yet how many Christians, in full knowledge of the truth, continue to nourish and cherish secret sins, embryonic creatures that can only destroy us in the end! Such sins, often condoned as "weaknesses," grow like the young cowbird until they choke out the tender fruits of the Spirit, eventually leaving us barren and forlorn, wondering why our hearts and lives are joyless and empty.

The faithful little vireo has no way of knowing what she is doing when she broods a cowbird in her nest. We have the clear guidance of the Word of God for our inner lives. When we sin, we sin in the presence of the Holy Spirit. Let us ask Him to search us and try us, to see if there is any wicked way in us, to root out of our minds and affections all that has not been placed there by the Lord Jesus, that we may bring forth fruit to His holy name!

vireo

Loon

The ice was barely out of the river when the high, thrilling calls of migrating loons began to sound overhead as they left their winter homes along the east and west seacoasts of the continent and began to fan out across the country in a northerly direction, seeking the freshwater lakes and rivers by whose lonely shores they would nest and rear their young.

They flew with legs extended and protruding beyond their short, stubby tails, their ponderous heads held lower than their bodies, their sturdy wings beating rhythmically at speeds that sometimes exceeded sixty miles an hour, their wild, free trumpeting filling the frosty skies gloriously from time to time. Now and again a pair would touch down to feed, landing with a long, low glide on the water, their heavy body-impact leaving a noisy trail of shining spray far behind.

It was then that their beauty could be seen most clearly — the straight, sharp bill, the black, velvety head plumage with its greenish gloss, the incomplete white collar, the white bar across the throat, the boldly checkered black and white back, the snowy underside visible only as they groomed themselves, rolling over on one side and working vigorously at their undercovering while one foot waved ludicrously in the air. Sometimes they would rear up on the water, stretch their necks, shake their heads, flap their wings vigorously as if getting ready to take off, and then settle back down again. What majestic creatures they were as they floated serenely on the still-icy waters!

Takeoff was something to see. Unable to rise in flight from land at all, loons have all they can do to mount the air even from water, so adapted are their bodies to swimming and diving. They would make many starts, half-running, half-flying along the surface of the water for anywhere from twenty

20

yards to a quarter of a mile, wings flapping violently, water splashing loudly all the while, sometimes calling as they went. Airborne at last, they would disappear into the distance, their familiar, distinctive outline fading — always flying north.

My loons returned as usual to the rocky, bare outcropping that broke water just off the shore of the river, not one hundred feet from my picture window; and on that barren island, not more than two feet from the water's edge, they pulled together the few bits of decaying vegetation that satisfied their instinct and served them as a nest. Within a day or two, they were incubating two precious eggs.

For nearly a month they tended their makeshift nest, the two parent birds sharing equally in the task. There were days of lashing wind and rain and high waters when I felt sure the eggs must be submerged or swept away. But amazingly they were kept warm, dry, and safe by the sitting parent. The other bird would fish nearby, diving deep below the icy surface to procure just the right kind of fish and crustaceans for their needs, his strong, short legs propelling him underwater with incredible speed and strength, occasionally using his wings to execute a swift turn.

The air echoed and reechoed with glorious mating calls, as day after day the two loons tended their nest. They had several distinct cries — a wild, excited laughter, a high, sustained trilling, a weird

loon

yodeling, and eeric, wolflike wail. All of them thrilled me to my being's core.

About the twenty-ninth day the eggs hatched, and two tiny chicks were tended lovingly by their devoted parents. The natal down was scarcely dry before the family abandoned the nest and the mother lifted the youngsters to cuddle among the soft feathers of her back instead.

Loons' legs are set so far rearwards on their heavy-headed bodies that they are able to walk on land only by doing a sort of awkward shuffle, breasts dragging along the ground, shoving their way to the water rather than walking the short distance from their nests to the shoreline. It was in this manner, on the morning after the eggs had hatched, that mother loon propelled herself to the edge of the outcropping and began to swim, babies safely stowed on her broad black-and-white back. I watched in utter fascination as the little ones rode high, dry, and safe on their living luxury-liner.

And then it happened. As I watched, my delight gave way to a cry of horror. For suddenly, in the manner of loons, mother submerged. The two tiny chicks, not yet twenty-four-hours old, were on their own in the cold, hostile water.

For a second they disappeared, but only for a second. Before the echo of my involuntary ex-clamation had died away, there were the chicks swimming busily about, their proud parents float-ing lovingly alongside. By the rude shock of being ducked, the young loons had come to discover their natural habitat, that environment in which they would flourish and rejoice for the rest of their lives.

And shall God deal with His children less lovingly, less wisely, or less faithfully than mother loon with her new chicks?

Habitat

She was a beginning bird watcher, and I had sent her a field guide as a gift. She wrote her thanks from northern Michigan where she was vacationing — an ideal spot for bird-watching if ever there was one.

"We were driving along a paved road the other day," she recounted happily, "and a mother loon with six little loons following her walked across the road just ahead of us, going into the woods from the lake. She looked just like the picture in your book."

I smiled. I did not think too hardly of my friend, for bird-watching is an exquisite and intricate art and one not learned overnight. I don't know what it was that she saw, but I do know that it was not a loon. For one thing, a pair of loons produce only two young in a season. For another, loons are water birds and have no interest whatsoever in the woods. And in the third place, loons are unable to walk on land. It is all they can do to shove themselves with an awkward, rolling shuffle the scant two or three feet to the water from their nest, which is built always as close to the shoreline as safety will permit.

evening grosbeak

Loons enjoy two natural habitats, but land is not one of them. Equally at home in the water or in the air, they are totally unable to cope with life on land; yet no bird is more gloriously free and at one with his true environment than a swimming or an airborne loon.

All living things, including man himself, can exist only in a particular environment. A study of habitat and the ways in which each species is adapted to life in its own element is both fascinating and rewarding.

Each kind of bird has its own feeding patterns and must live where its food can be found. Each breeds in a certain manner, and this, too, helps determine where it must live and how. Certain requirements of temperature must be met: a tropical bird cannot live in the Arctic, nor a snowy owl on the equator. And many saltwater birds would die if restricted to freshwater lakes and rivers.

Many adaptations must be served. Birds' feet are large or small, strong or weak, according to the way they

lesser yellow-legs

must be used. They are toed, webbed, clawed or taloned to satisfy the needs of walking, wading, swimming, perching, hovering, or carrying prey. Bills are short or long, conical, crossed, stubby or sharp, hooked or hammer-headed, curving or straight, whiskered or hypodermic–syringelike in order to crush grain, pick up tiny seeds, extract seeds from pine cones, secure almost invisible aerial insects, dig in the earth or under bark, catch and carry home fish, tear apart flesh, bore into trees, or suck nectar from flowers. Legs range in length according to use, from the extremely tiny weak ones of the hummingbird to the stiltlike legs of the waders. Body shapes and sizes, kinds and colors of feathers, contours of wings and

osprey

tail, variety and position of ears, eyes, and even, as in the case of the loon, legs — all are adapted to the habitat and life style of the species.

Courting and mating rituals vary according to the habitat, and so does the building of nests. Some birds build no nest at all, merely laying their

24

eggs on bare ground or barren rock. Others create nests of incredible delicacy and design, hanging them high on a swaying bough or low in a clump of weeds, hiding them deep on the forest floor or out in a grassy meadow. Some birds rear their young in a tiny cradle swinging from a slender branch overlooking water, while others brood in a lonely eyrie on a bleak mountaintop. A lifetime could be spent studying the amazing ways in which wild things seek their own environment and adapt their bodies and their lives to its requirements.

When a bird has found the habitat wherein by ceaseless endeavor it is possible for him to meet all his necessary needs, that bird will flourish, for he is functioning in his true environment. There and there only will he nest and produce his young; there alone will he know freedom, joy, and total harmony throughout all his being. In total fusion with his world, he finds his destiny — total fulfillment of that for which he was made.

Man's natural environment is God. If we would realize that destiny for which we were created and redeemed, we must find it in God through Jesus Christ. Nowhere else can we ever be truly and completely at home. Why is it that we are so much slower than God's feathered children to realize and adapt to our soul's true habitat?

Song Sparrow

Sometimes I like to take my boat and wander off to parts of the river where variations in habitat make it possible to see or hear birds not commonly found along my own stretch of shore.

Early one June morning I glided into a shallow backwater surrounded by deep forest. As always, I could hear more than I could see; I was soon aware of the presence of wild things not to be found in my own light bush and rock-strewn, swiftly flowing waters.

With a startled squawk a great blue heron rose on silent wing, disappearing over the treetops, flying with long, slow, gracefully measured beat, head drawn back on his breast, long legs trailing. The nasal "Yank! yank!" of a red-breasted nuthatch sounded urgently from afar; the hollow, wooden clucking of a black-billed cuckoo rattled eerily from some alders by the water.

High overhead a warbling vireo burst into song, his lovely, liquid phrases incredibly beautiful. Hidden in the forest floor, an artless wood thrush poured out his fluted melody, his pure, clear notes mounting the air like ever-increasing arcs of burnished gold. The bold, bright whistle of an oriole rang out to his nesting mate as he rejoiced again and again in the wonder of new life. From far away came the plaintive, serene sweetness of the song of a white-throated sparrow. In a clearing on the edge of the wood a purple finch sang in an ecstasy of abandon, as if all known joys were his and must be expressed in his song. And high in the branches overhead the shy, sweet piping of a reflective chickadee mingled with the soft, rhythmic tapping of a woodpecker.

I listened for an hour, then started home. Why are the finest singers always somewhere else? I mused as I passed an open stretch alive with the music of indigo buntings and goldfinches. Why

26

song sparrow

did my rocky acre seem to have so little of the glory that had refreshed and delighted me here?

As I turned into my own little cove and moored the skiff, suddenly a song sparrow at my side released a rivulet of sparkling crystal song on the morning air. Again and again he sang, as if his little heart would burst. "Sweet, sweet, sweet, oh, sweet, sweet!" he caroled. "Sweet, sweet, sweet!" What could have been more beautiful?

My heart was filled with shame. Here he lived, at my very door, singing his vibrant, heartwarming song from dawn to dusk. A tiny brown creature, so drab as to be almost invisible among the twigs and grasses where he makes his home, he lives modestly and happily in almost any terrain, ceaselessly ministering grace to all who have ears to hear.

Every habitat must by its very nature exclude many of birdland's most gifted choristers. We must travel about from spot to spot if we would hear their magnificent music or hope to view their vivid, flashing wings. But the homely song sparrow with his tiny, throbbing throat spreads beauty and joy, courage and hope almost everywhere.

We may not all have opportunity to thrill

daily to the songs of nature's most exotic singers, but God has left few of us without His song sparrows. May we become aware of them and learn to listen to their message with gratitude and thanksgiving!

Hummingbird

That tiniest sprite of the north woods, the ruby-throated hummingbird, has hovered about wildflowers along the river as long as I have been coming here, as well as about my garden in the city; but it was not until a year ago that I saw my first nest and sitting hen. And one holy morning, rapt with wonder, I held a delicate hummingbird in my hand.

Early in May, while it was still too cold for the flowers or insects which are its food, the infinitesimal creatures, scarcely larger than good-sized moths, returned from their winter home in Central America. How their gossamer wings carried them safely all those miles and how they charted their course, no one knows. But within days a homesite had been chosen and the female was busily at work constructing her nest.

She chose a slim branch about fifteen feet up a young birch tree that leaned well out across the water. There she created a neat cup out of bud scales and plant down, covering the outside with bits of lichen, binding it together and fastening it to the limb with spider silk. When I saw it in early July, it was about the size and color of a small walnut, and she was raising her second brood in it. To see that lovely creature, herself smaller than my thumb, sitting on her almost invisible nest, warming her eggs with her soft breast, head protruding slightly from one side of the nest, tail from the other, was a most moving sight.

Two tiny white eggs were incubated by the mother alone for sixteen days, while father disported himself about the bush, resplendent in his ruby-throated finery, seemingly without a care in the world.

She fed the nestlings on regurgitated, pre-digested food from her own crop, ramming her long, needlelike bill down their little gullets so insistently that I expected it to go right through nestlings and nest alike.

Finally the babies appeared, green like their mother, incredibly tiny and fragile-looking. Yet in a few weeks those mites would journey under their own wing power all the way to the tropics!

Some years before I had learned to feed hummingbirds by placing a solution of sugar and water in a small bottle and tying it to a bush with a brightly colored ribbon. Attracted by what seemed to be a flower, and finding nectar there, the little creatures would come to drink. But that year I did better — I bought two hummingbird feeders, tied them to a hemlock branch just outside my window, and waited to see how long it would take for the fledglings to learn to cross the river and locate them.

Two days later I found two birds almost too tiny to be seen poised on delicate, swiftly moving wings, their bills thrust into the feeders, drinking deeply. From then on they came several times a day — first the family from across the river, then, as it was possible to see by distinguishing differences in size and coloration, others as well.

What a thrill it was to see these exquisite birds only a few inches away and under the heavy magnification of binoculars! The iridescent green of their back feathers glowed like a thousand jewels in the sunlight; their graceful bodies were poetry in motion; their brilliant black eyes looked calmly into mine as they fed. The shimmering wings moved so rapidly that only a faint haze was visible as they hovered, flew forward, sideways, and occasionally even backward for a few moments.

The whirring of these rapidly pulsing wings gives the hummingbird its name. It has been estimated that their wings move ninety or more beats a second and can travel at a speed of thirty miles per hour. A thousand flowers a day must be visited in order to sustain such phenomenal activity, and the food is metabolized almost instantly.

Frequently I would see a tiny body perched on a twig, resting; but such a sight would last only a short time, for the feet and legs of this active mite are too undeveloped to allow it to perch for more than a few moments at a time. It is always a thrill to catch a glimpse of this tiniest of all bird profiles momentarily at rest!

The gay Lothario, he of the gleaming ruby throat, did not come to the feeders often, but roved the woods in total unconcern for his family and their doings. As the summer progressed, the juvenile males began to take on a faint flush of rose about the throat. By next year, they would return as adult males.

Then one morning as I rounded the corner of the cottage, I saw a tiny, inert green body lying on the ground below the picture window. With an exclamation of sorrow I stooped to pick up the almost weightless form, thinking to save it the final indignity of being eaten. As my fingers closed round it, I sensed an almost imperceptible heartbeat: the little creature was merely stunned, not dead. Gently I massaged the tiny breast with my thumb, warming the bird with my fingers and crooning to it. How exquisite were its jeweled feathers! How clearly the minute tips of black and white showed on the fine green tail-feathers! With what awe I held the lovely creature in my hand!

In a few minutes it opened its bright black eyes; its body relaxed and moved slightly in my hand. It rested awhile, then finally opened its long, slender bill, displaying an incredibly slim and flexible tongue. "Eeeeeeeh!" it murmured softly and moved its wings. I released it, and it flew safely

hummingbird

to a low branch. Within minutes it was hovering at the feeder, drinking deeply.

So many feathered visitors came to my feeders that despite my best efforts there were times when the vials would be empty for a few hours. Then my little friends would set about finding me to remind me of their needs, flying from window to window, looking in every room, tapping the glass gently if they saw me. If this did not locate me, they would search the nearby woods, the dock and boat, the sundeck, even the spot where I customarily swam, until they found me. Then they would dive-bomb me, whizzing by so closely at high speeds that my hair would be stirred by the breeze they created, or the pages of my book would rustle, and I would hasten to fill their feeders. When I had to be away for a week in August, they reproached me bitterly on my return. They also left a dozen small, neat holes in the screen nearest their feeders to remind me to take my responsibilities more seriously in the future.

As I write, another generation of hummingbirds is buzzing about me. The same parents returned and have placed their new nest on exactly the same spot in the same birch tree and are now on their second brood again. Within hours of arrival they were drinking at my feeders, already filled and waiting for them. How can they distinguish and find again their former breeding spots? No one knows, but it is a common thing among many species of birds.

If the tiny hummingbird knows enough to seek out the source of his food supply and make his wants clearly known, what about God's children? The ruby-throats seem to enjoy my feeders, and I love to have them around and observe them at close range. But they can get along without my aid and live quite adequately on their natural diet of nectar, insects, and sap from holes drilled by sapsuckers. We, however, have no resources of any kind apart from God. Shall we not come to Him as He has bid us come in His name — asking, seeking, knocking — that we may experience the abundance of His never-failing supply in every area of our lives?

Hummingbird

Small jeweled creature
   hovering close to Loveliness
flitting about in the sunshine
   now here,
     now there,
   on singing, iridescent wings
sipping daintily
   at the Source of all Sweetness
attracted to Beauty
   drawn by the warmth
   by the glow and glory of color
the fragility
   of delicately chiseled, brilliantly hued petal
   the clear, cold crystal of a dewdrop:

Do you drink at the Fountain
   deeply,
     thirstily
finding there sustenance
   life-giving
     soul-satisfying

Or do you really feed elsewhere
   on the grubby bark
   of an oak trunk
using the nectar of God's grace
   only as lovely, liquid effervescence?

Bluebird

Only once in my life have I seen a bluebird in its natural nesting habitat. One long-ago July, years before I had found my own spot on the river, I spent a month in a farming area in eastern Ontario. Snake fences and old, decaying apple trees provided what I now know is the true habitat of the bluebird — an environment that has all but disappeared in these days of wire fences and efficient, mechanized farming. Walking the dusty mile to the mail box each day, I would pass a field where, if fortune favored me, from a corner where two broken-down fences of ancient cedar rails met there would flash forth the shining arc of a bluebird, frequently singing as he mounted the summer air.

The jeweled luster of those glistening wings, touched to rainbow-hued brilliance by the afternoon sun, is with me today some forty years later, as real as if it were yesterday.

When I became a bird watcher, I wondered if I should ever see a bluebird again, for they have become all but extinct in my part of the world due to destruction of their native habitat; but about five years ago I made my first visit to Florida during a Christmas vacation. Bird-watching friends there were anxious to know if there was any one thing I particularly wanted to see. Knowing that the bluebird is sometimes found in Florida in the winter, I replied, "Bluebirds, if you know where we might find some!" Off we went to a rural area, not so different from the one where I had witnessed such incredible beauty so many years before; and sure enough — within half an hour we had seen two pair of the lovely creatures.

Three years later at my home in suburban Toronto, I had the astonishing experience of having nine or more bluebirds linger about my ravine-side garden for two full weeks during fall bluebird

migration. They were exceedingly tame, even perching unconcernedly on the windowsill not three inches from me as I sat in my living room, scarcely able to believe the wonders that my senses were telling me were true. Naturalists have been putting out nesting-boxes for bluebirds for some years, seeking to lure them back to Ontario where they were once so plentiful. Obviously they are meeting with success, for almost every autumn now the fall migration brings a few bluebirds to my door. One summer I even saw a fledgling, proving that there must have been a bluebird nest somewhere in my own ravine in the heart of metropolitan Toronto. I rejoice in the goodness of God for giving me the privilege of observing these exquisite creatures so closely.

The world views bluebirds as elusive symbols of happiness, like mythical phantoms to be pursued but never really grasped. I know that bluebirds, though rare, are real. I see them as God's messengers to His wayfaring pilgrims, speaking of promise, of hope, and of the golden summer of eternal joy that is the sure inheritance of those who love and trust Him.

Many Sparrows

I was grown-up before I knew there were any sparrows other than the so-called house sparrow or English sparrow. In the large city where I was raised, these noisy, quarrelsome little birds abounded, for they like to make their homes around the haunts of men. They are not sparrows at all, really, but weaver finches; and they are not native to North America. Like the starling, they were brought here by early colonists from Europe who thought they needed them in their new home.

If the homesteaders needed the house sparrow, the native birds here did not. The newcomers throve and in no time at all had spread wherever man was found in the new world; and as settlement spread farther west, so did the sparrows, driving away native songbirds and usurping their nesting cavities. The introduction of the weaver finch into this part of the world was a sad mistake.

But the native sparrows of North America, the only ones who are rightly called by the name of sparrow here — that's another thing. Our real sparrows are among the most beneficial of all our birds, not only consuming vast quantities of weed seeds and harmful insects, but ranking among our finest singers as well.

Sparrows are members of the large family of *Fringillidae*, to which grosbeaks, finches, and buntings belong, as well as about thirty varieties bearing the name of sparrow. All are seed eaters, although many species also eat insects, and the young are fed insects exclusively while in the nest. All bills are stout, conical in shape, and hard, suited to crushing seeds.

Gradually I became acquainted with the members of the sparrow family as my knowledge of birds expanded. I shall never forget the first time I heard and saw a song sparrow singing his heart out for joy one bitter March morning. His music and that of his ubiquitous and prolific clan never fails to thrill me to this day. Not all members of the sparrow family are beautiful singers, but many of the finest musicians of birdland are numbered among their ranks. And even the homely lisping of its less-well-endowed singers is cheerful, contented, and uplifting. The song sparrow, fox sparrow, and lark sparrow can hold their own in any group of songsters, while the sweet, plaintive call of the whitethroat is a deeply stirring experience to hear.

Most sparrows are ground dwellers and ground feeders, nesting on or very close to the ground. I have never been able to discover a nest, even though I have known they were about, so skillfully are they built and concealed. But I have known a song sparrow, for whom I laid a daily table of birdseed on a rock beside the river, to stamp her little foot loud enough for me to hear if I was late in getting her breakfast out.

Most sparrows perch to sing, mounting anything from a tall weed or a low shrub or fence wire to the highest treetop. They abound almost everywhere — in fields, swamps, and meadows, in light brush or in the deep woods, north of the Arctic Circle and well down into the southern United States, in marshes or by dusty roadsides, on the prairies or by the sea, in trees or shrubs, in gardens and hedgerows — wherever you may be you are likely to find some members of the sparrow family nearby.

To the uninitiated eye they all look alike — drab, brownish, nondescript little creatures, colored so like the grasses or dead leaves they frequent that it is easy to overlook them altogether. But with some time in the field, a good illustrated bird guide, and a pair of binoculars, distinguishing features will gradually emerge — a white throat here, a black-and-white or black-and-yellow striped crown there, wing bars on one, a rufous cast to the feathers of another, a striped breast, clear breast, or breast with a center spot on this one, pink legs with black feet on that, an upper and a lower mandible of different colors on the one bird, yellow lores on another, a rusty cap on that, here a rounded tail, there a forked one, or a tail with two white outside feathers.

And so you come to know the various sparrows: song sparrow, swamp sparrow, white-throated and white- or golden-crowned sparrows, savannah sparrow, tree sparrow, vesper sparrow, grasshopper sparrow, field sparrow, chipping sparrow, clay-colored sparrow, sage sparrow, sharptailed sparrow, and many more. Before long you will find yourself noting their songs, from the grasshopper-like buzz of the sparrow that bears that name to the sweet, flutelike piping of the singing sparrows.

So many sparrows! How difficult it is to learn to differentiate between them speedily and accurately, to catch the swift movement and graceful, undulating flight of each! Yet Jesus has told us that not one sparrow falls to the ground without God's noting it. We might be able to understand such a statement had He been speaking of some of

white-throated
sparrow

our brilliantly colored birds — the scarlet flash of a falling tanager or cardinal might well be visible, even to us. But a sparrow — that tiny, hard-to-see creature!

Why, then, should we fear? For God's children are of more value to Him than many sparrows.

Chickadee

What shall I say about this merry elf, flitting so gaily about the woodland, announcing his presence by his lighthearted, ringing call, "Chick-a-dee-dee-dee-dee!" or, less frequently, by the sweet, confiding two-note whistle that is his true song? More experienced ears can detect his nearness by the high, scarcely audible sibilance that sounds roundabout when this mischievous prankster wishes to arouse interest while still remaining entirely hidden.

Except in nesting season, chickadees are usually seen in small companies and are frequently accompanied by a loosely knit group of kinglets, nuthatches, and woodpeckers. The woods may ring with soft little sounds and yet nothing be visible, for these small creatures reveal themselves when and how they will.

Chickadee himself, however, is a trusting, friendly fellow, easy to distinguish with his saucy black bib and cap against white cheeks, his grey underparts edged with buffy-tangerine, and his greyish-white wing and tail feathers. He is a beautiful bird; but it is the impact of his shy, inquisitive, humorous, tantalizing personality that will make your friendship with a chickadee such a warm, rewarding experience. Few birds are quite as engaging as the black-capped chickadee and his southern cousin, the tufted titmouse.

He is among the easiest of all birds to attract to a feeder, and it is there that most of my intimate acquaintances with chickadees have occurred. Being permanent residents in northern climates, chickadees will feed freely on suet during the cold weather; but sunflower seeds at any season will send a chickadee straight into bird paradise. I keep half a dozen feeders filled with these around my river property, not that the birds need the food in summer so much as that I need the birds. They visit me in groups of from five to thirty-five several times a day.

Chickadees are gregarious little fellows and seem to enjoy having me watch them as they savor their sunflower seeds. They will call me with their sibilant lispings, remaining hidden until they know they have fully engaged my attention.

Occasionally in excitement some youngster shrilly calls out "Chickadee-dee-dee-dee!" as if to tell me where I should look. But usually there is only the sibilance until suddenly, with a special whirring of wings seemingly reserved for occasions such as this, a bird will whizz past me, changing course just in time to avoid hitting me, followed by several of his companions all making similar dive-bombing expeditions. They will then settle down to the serious business of feeding, whisking the seeds one by one into nearby branches for husking and eating, then zooming down for more. It is highly entertaining, as well as surprisingly moving, to watch a flock of chickadees feeding.

The chipmunks try to raid my feeders, for they, too, adore sunflower seeds, and a great battle of wits takes place between us as I seek to protect my feeders — with considerably less than 100 percent success I might add. At one time I wondered how the furry fellows knew what toothsome treasures lay hidden in the odd-looking assortment of rusty salmon tins, coconut half-shells, and other strange devices swinging at the end of fine copper wire suspended from second wires strung between two trees. I found out one day when I saw a chickadee toss a few seeds from his aerial feeder squarely at a chipmunk, deliberately tantalizing him. Within a day or two every chippy in the neighborhood was gathered below the feeders

chickadee

42

whenever they heard the chickadees' soft sighing in the trees. Usually a few seeds were tossed down to them, and these would be caught before they reached the ground.

Heaven help me if the food supply runs low. Scolding chickadee calls will alternate with the beguiling entreaties of their sweet whistled song. If I am outside, wings will flutter and whirr all about me. If I am indoors, the windows will be buzzed alarmingly, and on occasion I have been aroused by the sharp tapping of a stout little beak on the glass. My chickadees seldom come in for breakfast much before mid-morning, obviously having other important business to attend to earlier in the day, but when they arrive they expect breakfast to be not only ready, but plentiful!

What have I learned from my love affairs with the chickadee tribe? Nothing spectacular, perhaps. But in them I see revealed daily more and more of the greatness and the goodness of my God. Is not this reward enough?

Night Watch

It was a brilliant moonlit night in early July. About midnight I took the boat and slipped around to a quiet backwater where I could enjoy the glory of the night skies unhampered by the house lights that dimmed their beauty along the main channel of the river.

Newly risen, the moon was full, picking out the birches in the deep forest along the shores and touching each with an other-earthly silver radiance. Behind them, towering beech and maple mingled with pine, spruce, and hemlock loomed in black relief. Not a leaf stirred; the silent forest, broken here and there by a jagged outcropping of ancient rock, was mirrored back, motionless, in the still waters. Only my paddle moved.

I glided to the spot where I tied up when I came back here to watch an oriole's nest, which I had been doing daily for the past two weeks. I made the boat fast to a stump protruding from the water near the beaver lodge and lay back luxuriously to give myself to the unbroken contemplation of the starry heavens spread before me as if in the loveliness of their primeval hour. In so doing, I inadvertently sent a beam from my flashlight through the birch that housed the orioles.

In the split second before I heard the quick rush of startled wings, I caught a fleeting glimpse of the bright breast of father oriole. He had been roosting on the branch beside his precious nest

Baltimore oriole

44

where his faithful mate was incubating their eggs. With a frightened flutter he fled into the forest. I quenched the light and sat in repentant silence. In less than a minute he recovered from his shock and slipped back again to take his place of guard beside his nest. Gradually a shining shaft of moonlight picked out his bright plumage, and he was still to be seen keeping watch over his loved ones when I left an hour later.

How safe are the hearts and the homes that are watched over by the covenant care of the eternal Father who, watching over His children, neither slumbers nor sleeps!

High Noon

There had been unbroken heat for several days that July. I laid aside my writing at midmorning one day, packed a lunch, and set off downriver to do some bird-watching for a while.

I had not gone far before I realized that it was hotter in my open boat on the water than it had been at my typewriter on the veranda. It was breathlessly still, not a leaf moving, the water motionless except where my bow cut through it. At its zenith now, the sun beat down mercilessly, casting no shade anywhere.

I knew there would be little bird activity at noon on such a hot day and toyed with the idea of turning back. But some restlessness made me keep going despite the heat.

A couple of miles downstream I turned into a long, shallow bay, its waters starred with white lilies and treacherous with deadheads. It was unsafe to use the motor here, so I began to paddle, finding the light exertion almost intolerable in the heat. I was heading for an old dam half a mile farther on where herons and other waterfowl were often to be found. I paddled slowly, hugging the shore in the futile hope of finding a little shade, scanning the shores as I went.

My fears were correct; certainly there was no movement in the woods that noon. Any bird who had found a cool roost in a shady tree had enough sense to stay there.

All but one, that is. My binoculars picked up a spot of brilliant color at the water's edge, but nothing seemed to be moving. My pulses quickened as they always do at an unexpected discovery. What was it? I wondered, paddling closer to the shore.

Before long I was near enough to see it clearly without the binoculars. There stood a gorgeous male oriole, his orange breast and rich black head blazing in the noonday sun, alternately bathing, wading, and quenching his thirst. He surveyed me calmly for a moment, then went tranquilly about his business.

I watched him for about half an hour, engrossed in the lovely sight, the heat forgotten. I had never seen an oriole bathe before, and the combination of his vivid colors against the rich green of the woods and the deep blue of the river made a truly unforgettable picture. When I started home a while later, it was with a sense of refreshment and release.

Just as uniquely, in the midst of the heat of the day God sends some token of His love and care to refresh the weary hearts of His children. A remembered verse of Scripture, the words of a hymn, a phone call from a friend, an unexpected sense of His presence, a sudden answer to some prayer, a song of praise — these He sends, His oriole at high noon, to cheer His pilgrims on their way.

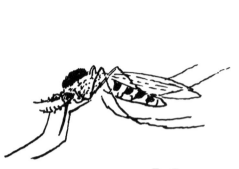

Mosquitoes

Lord, Your mosquitoes
  are driving me crazy tonight!
I try to rest
  here in this woodland spot,
so quiet, so lovely,
  so filled with Your tranquillity —
but rest I cannot
  for this buzzing throng
of tiny, needled dive-bombers
  all declaring war
      on me.

If only they would bite me and have done!
  But no, they whine,
hovering near and nearer,
  then receding,
only to reappear
  just as I start to drowse.
I slap, and miss,
  thoroughly roused;
they sting, and then make off,
  only to renew the attack
      from another direction.

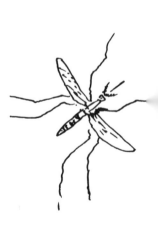

Lord, why did You make mosquitoes,
　　the serpent in this paradise of beauty?

Hush! It was man that sinned,
　　and nature fell perforce;
Nature that still awaits
　　with earnest expectation
the redemption of our body,
　　when it, too, shall be freed
　　　　from sting of sin.

And in the meantime, I have made mosquitoes
　　and other noxious insects
to serve as food
　　for orioles.

Goldfinch

How like living sunbeams are these lovely little creatures of the humblest meadows, road sides, or gardens! Merry singing sprites clad in butter yellow with neat black trim, they flit in and out of our ordinary days like the promises of God, cheering our hearts, lifting our eyes heavenwards, and giving promise of blessings yet to come — little thoughts of God sent down to us to touch the commonplace of earth with the radiance of the eternal.

I was walking in an open ravine early one August morning when I heard the music of a host of bird voices borne towards me on the shining air. Rounding a bend in my path, I found myself in a sheltered valley where before my delighted eyes were spread several hundred male goldfinches clinging to the sow thistle plants which seemed to stretch endlessly before me, gathering their silky down and filling the air with glorious song. What a sight to experience! What a song to remember! Such a number of goldfinches gathered together is called a charm, and how utterly appropriate is the word!

Goldfinches do not nest until the sow thistle provides them with its silk to line their nests and its seed to feed their young. They have been known to nest as late as October, but August is the more likely month. So it was that one August at the river I witnessed a goldfinch singing his mating song — a long, liquid stream of crystal and gold being flung forth from the tip of the highest tree he could find. Unlike his gay flight song with its short, melodic phrases, this song went on and on and on as if the tiny, pulsing body contained enough rapture to flood the whole universe with his joy. Certainly it flooded my day with happiness even though it got me out of bed at 5:00 A.M.; and even now I recall it with wonder and awe.

goldfinch

One of the most charming sights I have ever been privileged to behold took place while a friend's houseboat was tied up by the swing bridge some miles upriver and we were picnicking along the rocky shore. A goldfinch had decided that hot August afternoon to take a bath just a few feet from where our table was spread. Tiny as he was, he found himself a secluded spot just his size and waded in up to his knees — all of half an inch. Then with joyous abandon he began to dance up and down in the cool water, spreading his wings, riffling his feathers, splashing water over himself, enjoying himself to the full. Indeed, so absorbed did he become in his delights that he quite forgot that the river is a through waterway used by boats of all kinds, but especially by large cruisers which charge up and down at high speeds throwing enormous wakes to either side.

And that was what happened now. A huge wave spewed out by a racing cruiser caught the little fellow unawares, sweeping him off his feet, tumbling him over and over in its undertow before finally receding and dying away along the shores. The tiny creature extricated himself with a somewhat dazed expression, hopped onto a rock, shook himself thoroughly, then stepped down to the water's edge, looked upriver and down, then calmly went on with his bathing. Soon his sweet, piping song sounded cheerily from overhead as he flew off to feed along the roadside.

As I watched the goldfinch, so fragile yet so secure, I thought of the query of the ancient prophet — a question that all mortality must face sooner or later: "How wilt thou do in the swelling of Jordan?" (Jer. 12:5). For the trusting soul there need be no fear, for God Himself gives answer to His children: "When thou passest through the waters, I will be with thee; and through the rivers, they shall not overflow thee" (Isa. 43:2). Rejoice, then, "For the Lord shall be thy confidence, and shall keep thy foot from being taken" (Prov. 3:26).

Goldfinches

One summer morning,
wandering by a stream,
I chanced upon a valley
frosted with seeded silk
of dandelion and sow thistle.

Far as eye could see
a noxious silver stream
drifted the shining air towards the hilltop,
where patient toilers strove
to keep their gardens
free from weeds —
my own small plot was there.

I roamed an hour,
then, returning,
passing that way again,
I found the air
a-throb with fluted song.
The valley lay transfigured,
its seed pods blotted out
by the rich, pulsing gold and black
of myriad feeding finches.

Lord, have I been so careful
to weed the small discomforts, one by one,
from my life's garden,
that I have left no room for You
to heal my hurts,
to touch my grief with gold,
that I have missed the glory and the song
of Your goldfinches?

Silent Morn

A loved companion in my home, whether in the city or at the river, is Figaro, my dear black cat. In the nine years we have lived together, he has disclosed only one major fault to my devoted eyes — he stalks and eats birds. Although fed on the fat of the land, from kittenhood he has displayed an astonishing capacity for hunting and demolishing the other creatures I love — my birds. Various cats I have had have contented themselves with catching mice or chasing chipmunks. But almost from infancy Figaro caught birds, although he early learned not to let me see him doing it.

One morning the inevitable happened. Before my horrified eyes Figaro caught and ate my song sparrow. The poor distressed mate called and mourned for most of the morning, then lapsed into grieved silence.

Two or three kinds of singing sparrows nest about my cottage, usually raising two or three broods a year, so that the air is sweet with sparrow song most of the summer. But from the time the bereaved bird ceased its forlorn chipping, and for forty-eight full hours subsequently, not a sparrow raised its voice anywhere around me. All was silent; there was not even a sparrow to be seen. Whether birds really do mourn, do communicate their grief to others of their kind, or do withhold their songs for sorrow, I cannot tell. I only know the two-day silence I endured that July weighed so oppressively on my spirit that I was almost physically ill.

It is the nature of cats to kill birds. They cannot help it. We must not hold it against them:

we, too, kill to eat. Yet it can cause untold anguish to a sensitive spirit when one beloved creature who is our dear friend destroys another friend equally beloved.

What, then, must be the pressures on the heart of the Father when He sees His creatures, now no longer held captive to the downward pull of their own nature but richly endowed with the very nature of God through His Holy Spirit, seeking to destroy others equally gifted and beloved?

song sparrow

Cowbird

I was drifting about in the millrace behind the cottage one afternoon watching two nests I had been visiting daily. An oriole and a kingbird had built in the same tree, a slim young birch that leaned precariously out over the river. There were nestlings in the kingbird's nest, though the mother still appeared to be sitting on some unhatched eggs; as far as I could tell, the oriole was still incubating.

Both male birds were bustling about, calling to their mates, occasionally feeding them or relieving them on the nest, singing from time to time the loud, possessive song of mated birds — the oriole's song a lovely one, the kingbird's merely a noisy one.

Mrs. Oriole's task seemed to me to be the harder one, for while the kingbird could look out across the woods and water from her place on the nest and could see her mate on occasion, the oriole was hidden far in the depths of her pendant, basketlike nest where her eggs lay some six inches below the entrance level. It was only when the mother came to the top of the nest for a moment now and again that I could see her or that she had any view of the world outside.

Suddenly my ear was caught by a soft, high-pitched, hissing whistle above me. Looking up, I saw perched on the topmost bare branches of a large, lightning-killed pine tree four birds overlooking the two nests I was watching and probably several others as well. I scarcely needed to look at the quartet — their posture as well as their peculiar voices had identified them to me.

Two pair of cowbirds were watching the nests, hoping to catch one of the sitting mothers off-guard and lay one of their own eggs in her nest. For cowbirds are parasitic birds. They build no nests of their own, incubate no eggs. Not for them

the tedium
of foraging to
feed a nest
of young.
Instead,
they watch
the nests of
small birds,
particularly
warblers, vireos,
flycatchers, finches, and
thrushes, and lay their eggs
indiscriminately, one here, one
there, leaving them for the songbirds to hatch and raise.

cowbird

Sometimes the brooding mother manages to throw the strange egg from the nest; sometimes she even builds a new floor over the unwelcome egg and goes ahead with her own egg laying upstairs. Nests have been found having as many as six layers, each sealing off the egg of a cowbird, with the songbird's own family being successfully reared on the seventh level — the original high-rise apartment!

Far more often, however, the cowbird succeeds in her nefarious design. The little host accepts the egg as her own and incubates it. Cowbirds being a larger species than most of the birds chosen to mother them, the young are larger and stronger than the little songbirds. When the nest becomes crowded, the young interloper hurls the rightful nestlings to the ground, appropriating for itself all the space and all the food the mother brings. Though a cowbird will lay only one of its eggs in any given nest, that is frequently enough to destroy some or all of the host's family; and sometimes more than one cowbird will lay in the same nest, in which case the little songbirds must surely all perish.

Cowbirds belong to the blackbird family, though they have sparrowlike bills, short and stout rather than long and slender. The male has a glossy black body crowned with a brown head and brown eyes. The female is brownish-grey, rather a nondescript bird, with fine dark streaking on her underparts and a pale throat, usually unstreaked. Both birds are from seven to eight inches long.

And so the cowbirds kept their watch high above my nests, waiting for the unprotected moment when they could lay their parasitic eggs and disappear from the scene.

I know that the kingbird family throve; I watched the little ones learn to fly and hunt. I saw the two devoted orioles feed their nestlings for a few days, but I never saw a fledgling emerge from that beautiful, aerial nest, nor did I ever observe young orioles feeding or fluttering about in that vicinity, although the parent birds stayed around that part of the river for several weeks. Whether I just chanced not to see the young or whether they were destroyed by a young cowbird, I do not know; but I have a sick little feeling in my heart whenever I pass that softly swinging nest and remember the sharp-eyed watchers I had seen on the dead pine above it.

We, too, have an enemy who would rob us of the precious fruit of the Holy Spirit that God means all His children to have. Ever watchful, Satan seeks an unguarded moment wherein he can implant in our hearts and minds a seed of sin. A wrong thought, an unholy desire, a tiny dishonesty or bending of the truth, a yielding to a natural impulse, the cherishing of a grievance or brooding over a fancied slight — such things are the basis of secret sin which, if nourished, can only bring forth fruit unto death, robbing us of our power and leaving our lives joyless, barren, and empty.

How much we need the whole armor of God to enable us to stand against the wiles of the devil! And how infinite is the provision that our Savior has made for our needs, that we may be neither barren nor unfruitful in the knowledge of our Lord Jesus Christ (2 Pet. 1:3-8)!

A Merry Heart

I have never for a moment doubted that God has a wonderful sense of humor. He has made so many delightfully ludicrous creatures and situations and has placed such a sense of genuine fun deep within the hearts of all His animal kingdom, including mankind, that it is impossible to believe a sense of humor is anything but the joyous gift of an all-loving, all-wise Creator, sharing with His creatures this facet, too, of the totality of His own infinitely rich and full-orbed nature.

Nor are birds exempt from the common heritage. On many occasions I have had experiences with birds that can only be interpreted in the context of a joke.

How many times when in field or wood looking for birds to watch I have been made aware that there are really no bird watchers at all — only people watchers! Birds are infinitely more adept at watching us than the best of us are at watching them. They seem to enjoy putting us properly in our place by hiding in such a manner that it is impossible for us to see them, while they can watch us perfectly, chirping or otherwise making their presence known simply to tantalize us. Even my own little friends who come regularly to my feeders seem to like to sneak up behind me occasionally and say "Boo!" probably for the fun of making the bird watcher jump and look chagrined.

When loons are floating about on the river and all is quiet, I sometimes call to them in my version of loon language to see if they will answer. Sometimes they do, although frequently they will ignore my overtures. After we have carried on a little conversation, during which the loons will speak perfectly good loon sense while I probably babble utter nonsense, possibly even loon profanities, the birds will take off in a burst of wild, unrestrained laughter, or even worse, will sub-

merge to give way to their mirth in private. They do
not talk with me because they gain anything by it;
they merely indulge a foolish human, tolerantly
and benignly. But they can only take so much
human idiocy before dissolving in laughter.

Three different kittens I have owned have
been the butt of jokes played on them by a heron, a
woodpecker, and a pheasant respectively. Mehit-
able, my calico kitten, decided one day to stalk a
great blue heron who stood on one leg fishing in
the little bay beside the cottage. Slinking low on
her belly with all her eight-week-old skill, tail
twitching with desire, the tiny black and white and
orange atom worked her way down the hill to
where the bird stood motionless at the edge of the
water, head drawn back, seemingly oblivious to all
about him. When the kitten was within four feet of
him, slowly the bird drew himself up to his full
height, stretched his long neck to its limit, extended his wings to their full span of almost six
feet, opened his huge bill, and turned and looked at
the mighty hunter. With a terrified yelp the kitten
dashed for the shelter of my arms; and I heard that
heron chuckle as he flapped lazily away.

Likewise, tiny golden Impy decided to catch
a hairy woodpecker who was perching atop my
cedar flagpole. With a great show of bravado the bit
of fluff began to climb the thirty-foot pole, the
pecker watching quizzically out of one eye. He
remained motionless until she was about eight feet
above its rocky base; then suddenly he beat a re-
sounding tattoo with his hammer-headed bill on
the tinder-dry apex of the pole. The kitten dropped
like a bullet to the stones below and was still
trembling in my arms ten minutes later. And again
I heard a bird chortle with glee.

Figaro, in his brash youth, once undertook
to stalk a glorious cock pheasant who allowed him
to approach within a foot before puffing out his

copper-red breast and drumming his wings like a volley of thunder. Once again the kitten fled for refuge to my arms; and once again I heard that pheasant laugh as he skimmed off across the valley on derisive wing.

I remember the time I took thirty-eight nine-year-olds down a wooded ravine one afternoon in early spring to view the wonders unfolding that rainy April day. An early blue jay was calling from the leafless trees above us. Wherever we walked, he went, too, his calls becoming increasingly mocking in quality. For over an hour we wandered those wooded trails; for over an hour he jeered at us; yet not once did any one of our thirty-nine pair of eyes descry the prankster. "Yah — can't see me, can't see me!" he taunted us again and again, and he was right. We never did see him; and I can hear the echo of his rude laughter as I write today.

Crows and other large birds who raid the nests of smaller ones, devouring their eggs or their young, actually stand in secret fear of the songbirds they ravage. They know that their own eyes are vulnerable to the angry, darting bills of the tiny outraged parents and that a blind bird quickly becomes a dead one. Hence the robber flees at top speed, and it is not at all unusual to see a good-sized bird pursued by one or a pair of shrieking, dive-bombing small ones; more than one gangster has paid with his life for his nefarious thievery.

However, I once knew a crow and a pair of orioles who seemed to have worked out some sort of compromise in this matter and made a game of such a chase. Two or three times a day they would go streaking across the skies and valley beyond my picture window, the smaller birds in hot but apparently not angry pursuit. When they dropped behind in seeming weariness or flagging interest, the crow would slowly circle and give them oppor-

family to pace him again for a time, until finally they would call the whole thing off until later in the day, when they would renew it with fresh vigor. I watched these chases all through one June, and never once did I note any sign of real animosity between the birds. They seemed to engage in the battle simply for the fun of it.

I think that God plays His little jokes as well.

Among the most colorful and exquisite of all birds are the tiny members of the wood warbler family. These beautifully marked insect eaters of the northern woodlands glow with an almost etheral quality as they flit like burnished jewels among the treetops, delighting the eager eyes of only the most diligent and skilled of bird watchers, for they are difficult to see. One would expect that creatures so ravishing to the eye would delight the ear also, but almost none of them do. No member of the family warbles, though a few of them have quiet little songs, pleasant if rather hard to hear. The rest of them? Opening their dainty bills, they emit such an assortment of rasps, buzzes, wheezes, creaks, squeals, and other incongruous and inharmonious sounds as to be almost incredible. A

great blue heron

rusty hinge, a squeaky saddle, a rasping saw, a buzzing fly — these are the characteristic sounds of the lovely, elfin warbler family. I think God must have chuckled as He made the warblers in creation's dawning!

"He that is of a merry heart hath a continual feast," wrote the Wise One; "a merry heart doeth good like a medicine" (Prov. 15:15; 17:22). A gracious God has given to all His creatures the healing gift of laughter. It is good to share a joke with almighty God!

Bird Songs

Learning to recognize birds by their songs is a long and intricate business and one which I make no claim to having mastered. There are still far more bird songs that I don't know than those I can identify. However, I am learning, and each new conquest brings new joy. It adds to one's skill in birding, too, for if you know the name of the bird you hear, you will know where to look for it — high in the treetops, low in the brush, and so on — and so your sightings increase.

There are numerous good reasons why it is difficult to acquire skill in the recognition of songs. Many birds have more than one song: the cardinal, for instance, has several clearly distinguishable ones. All birds have an alarm note, most sounding much alike, as do their scolding notes. Most have at least one call as well as their song; some have several. Some birds seem able to practice ventriloquism, probably delighting in sending watchers off on wild-goose chases. Others can mimic — for the express purpose, I suspect, of bamboozling the unsuspecting listener. The mockingbird is nature's most accomplished mimic, having a phenomenal capacity for imitating not only the songs of scores of other birds, but sounds of every description. He is followed closely by the blue jay and the catbird: I once had a baby catbird sit on a low bough beside me and assure me solemnly that he was a bobolink!

Birds, like people, have local dialects; hence a song sparrow in New York may sound quite different from a song sparrow in Ontario. This is most frustrating to the beginning listener, although sooner or later he will learn to listen to the shape of a song, not just its particular notes. There is always the disarming chipmunk, too; though I know him well, his chipping has had me scanning the trees with my binoculars more times than I can number.

And there is always something new to learn. Only this morning while paying an early visit to a beaver meadow along the river where I have an oriole's nest to watch, I tried to track down a catbird calling from some low bushes. My attention was diverted by a pair of red-eyed vireos. Usually quite difficult to see, inhabiting the highest treetops, these two were flitting restlessly back and forth among low alders, and I seized the opportunity to study them. With part of my mind I noted that the catbird was moving about more than is customary. Eventually the truth dawned on me as I sighted one vireo in my glass and watched him utter the catbirdlike meowing sound again and again. When I looked up the vireo later, I found that in addition to his usual song he is credited with uttering "a long nasal quee" when disturbed. If I had not witnessed this, I would have no idea just what those words mean; but having seen and heard it, I will never forget it. Similarly, I first learned the sapsucker's mewing cry when tracking down what seemed to be a catbird.

Most bird songs are actually proclamations of territorial rights and are sung vigorously by the male from all precincts of his nesting area several times daily during the breeding season. Other males of the same kind know that they may not nest in his quarters, although birds of other species are free to do so. Basically, his assertion of ownership insures possession of an area that will contain enough of his particular kind of food to raise his family through the fledgling stage; and the size of the space he claims will vary according to the abundance or scarcity of the food supply that season.

When the young are fledged, there is less need for the protection of song, hence less singing. During the summer molt, when all migrants are getting new feathers to enable them to reach their winter homes, most songs cease altogether.

Not many females sing, though a few of them do. One of the most beautiful soloists I ever heard was a female oriole whom I observed singing her heart out in the top of my apple tree one sweet May morning.

Birds do sometimes converse together, usually in quiet, conversational tones; and frequently they will croon soft lullabies while sitting on their nests.

It is thought that in addition to declaring their territorial boundaries by song, many birds also sing for their own pleasure and that of their mates. Certainly their songs vary from hearing to hearing, being longer, shorter, more or less intricate and ornamented, and so on; and they sing more frequently, more beautifully and at greater length in good weather than in bad. Thrushes, for instance, sometimes sing in duet, seemingly for the pure joy of making music. One of the most profoundly moving experiences I have ever had came to me while sitting behind my cottage one afternoon in late July. Two wood thrushes, birds who usually sing only morning and night, only in nesting season, and only in the depths of the forest, had so far forgotten themselves as to sing a two-hour duet only a few yards away from my back door and treated me to the most sublime concert of bel canto singing I have ever been privileged to hear.

wood thru

All this means, however, that if certain birds do not nest in your locality, your chances of hearing them sing are very poor, although you may hear some singing during migration weeks.

The finest bird songs are sung from shortly before dawn until two or three hours after it; a repeat though abbreviated performance, seldom quite as lovely, takes place in the early evening. Birds sing in sequence, from the earliest to the latest risers, and wave after wave of new morning music breaks on the listening ear. In our workaday world it is not always possible to get out at the times the birds choose to command our presence, although most of us could get out more if we really desired to do so.

When we do, we usually suffer from an embarrassment of riches: everything sings at once, and it is next to impossible to isolate one song and learn it. If we do succeed in hearing one bird clearly above its fellows, we are little farther ahead — unless we can see the singer, we can't put a name to the song. How can one ever hope to become familiar with the myriad voices in the glorious chorus and find their tiny, elusive owners?

The study of bird records, along with their pictures, is a first step. Listen to them while doing routine tasks, and even though at first you may find them a bewildering jumble of similar sounds, gradually a few songs will lodge in your mind. Suddenly, one day, you will recognize a song in the field and be able, if not to name it on the spot, at least to remember it well enough to check with your records later. And someday you will be able to hear a song, many songs, and call each singer by name.

I have found that whenever I have the good fortune to see a bird while it is singing, I remember that song. Sitting quietly in the field or woods or drifting about on the river, every so often I will cight a bird while it is singing. As I become more adept at bird watching, these occasions occur more frequently. Working away at my records as well, I am slowly building up a repertoire of bird songs and calls that I really know, and my pleasure in birding is intensified for each new addition to the list. What joy it is to awaken to bird song and without going to the window to be able to name the morning songsters, or to walk in the woods, naming one by one the invisible choir overhead!

Have you ever wondered if, amid the confused babble of human prayers and cries ceaselessly ascending before Him, God can distinguish one voice from another — can really hear *your* call?

As I found how difficult it was to differentiate among bird songs and to learn to name the singers and listen to each song individually, a familiar word from the Scriptures took on new meaning for me. "I know thee by name," God said to Moses (Exod. 33:17). And to me, too, comes His promise: "Fear not: for I have redeemed thee, *I have called thee by thy name*; thou are mine" (Isa. 43:1).

What incredible wonder that the Creator and Lord of this infinitely vast universe should not only know His children, but know each one personally, each one by name!

Bird Whispers

It was not until I had a robin's nest in the big oak just outside my door that I learned about birds' whisper songs.

Sitting on the verandah watching the sun setting across the river in the hush of the evening, I would watch the mother bird go off for her final feeding of the day, then return and settle down for the night. For a moment the silent dusk would be shattered by the shrill voices of the youngsters clamoring for food; then all would be still again as the mother spread her wings in shelter over her brood. It was then that I first heard her sing her lullaby.

If I had not known the robin's song so well, I might never have connected the soft little murmur I heard with that particular bird; I would have considered it just one more of nature's sweet, nameless evening sounds. Indeed, the first several times I heard it, it did not really catch my attention at all. Then one night, shortly after mother robin had settled her babies to rest, I recognized the unmistakable shape of the robin's song in a low, humming croon, scarcely above a whisper, and I realized that it must be a sort of lullaby the mother bird was singing to herself. From then on, I listened carefully each evening. Sure enough, every night mother robin murmured her almost inaudible good-night song of joy and contentment, until not only were her little ones sleeping, but so was she.

Since then, I have heard birds of many varieties croon to their young and to each other and came to the conclusion that this is something a great many birds do, although only recently have I found this documented in bird literature. It is a beautiful and moving thing to hear.

A young fledgling, exploring his newly developing vocal powers, may sometimes be heard repeating his discoveries over to himself in a bird whisper, as though awed by the enormity of the powers he is finding within himself. Young birds murmur to each other as they learn to forage, and parent birds sometimes communicate with their little ones this way.

Watching an oriole's nest daily during incubation period this summer, I delighted in the glorious songs with which the devoted father would reassure and encourage his mate while she brooded her eggs hidden in the depths of her hanging nursery, suspended high above the river, often swaying none too gently in the wind. When he would see me moor my boat in a spot which he thought was a little too close to his treasures, however, he became visibly anxious. If he sang, he seemed to reason, he would betray the presence of his family; if he didn't sing, he would betray the confidence of his mate. He resolved his dilemma by singing sotto voce — by whispering his love to his mate, obviously hoping I would not be able to hear him.

Later when the young were fledged and he no longer carried so much responsibility for them, I would see him flitting about the treetops, foraging, usually accompanied by his mate, the youngsters feeding not far away. He would frequently hum a little tune to himself, barely audible but clearly an oriole song. Sometimes, preoccupied, he would murmur only the first two or three notes and then break off, sometimes continuing in a moment or so or sometimes abstractedly repeating the first phrase two or three times, for all the world like an absent-minded human being.

I have learned to hear and to recognize the fragmented song-whispers of many species of birds in the quiet of the woods around the river.

Sometimes a mated pair will speak their soft whispers of love and hope to each other, and this is an especially lovely thing to hear. Whispers can

72

robin

usually be heard just before dawn, as if the birds are murmuring sleepily to each other before awakening fully to burst into morning songs; although a friend who frequently walks a wooded road in the small hours of the night tells me that the woods are never really still — bird whispers may be heard at any hour of the night.

It took my ears some time to become attuned to hearing and distinguishing the whispered songs and conversations of birds, but when they did, it became an exciting and beautiful thing to overhear their sweet secrets. I came to know birds more intimately in this manner than when I had known them only in the glory of their full-orbed songs.

Sometimes an awareness of God's love comes to us like the joyous caroling of rich-voiced morning singing, as if everything around us were proclaiming His faithfulness, His love, and His care for His own. But God has His secrets, too, and "The secret of the Lord is with them that fear him; and he will shew them his covenant" (Ps. 25:14). He whispers His secrets to His children in a thousand ways, but only those whose ears are closely attuned to Him are aware of Him intimately, for He speaks in the stillness when other voices are silent. His voice may be heard in the darkness, giving songs in the night. With those who hear Him, He shares His counsels and the certainties of His covenant.

It is exciting and glorious beyond all words to listen to the whispered secret of almighty God! Who would not have his ears — more, his whole being — attuned to that still, small voice?

Waiting

The woods are still
   not the fall of a leaf
breaks the silence

   Bird song is hushed
Not a wing flits
   not a breath stirs

I sit and wait
   patient, unmoving
all the long
   silent morning
hoping to see Your glory
   revealed afresh
in flight and song of bird.

A slow hour passes
   and another
Not a bird shows
   The woods appear deserted

Yet well I know
   that brush and branch and tree trunk
teem with Your birds!

In silence and unseen
   they throng on every hand
close where I sit.

Although I see them not
   I know them near,
and know the woodland air
   will glow to their jeweled colors,
throb to their song,
   in their good time

I leave the wood, contented,
   knowing this

Your presence, Lord,
   the proving of Your power
the reality of Your promises,
   these, like the birds,
sometimes elude me
   seeming to be hid
when I wait for You.

Teach me to know
   that, like Your birds
silent and still in the leafy wood,
   Your glory and Your song are always there
waiting to be revealed
   in Your good time.

Migration

The mystery of bird migration has never been fully explained.

What prompts birds to leave a comfortable home and an abundance of food in a sunny clime and undertake a long, perilous journey north against heavy odds in order to nest and breed many hundreds, often thousands, of miles away? Most returning birds do so long before the weather is as warm or the food as plentiful as it is in their winter quarters; in fact, late spring snowstorms frequently result in starvation and death for many migrants each year.

Unnumbered perils attend migratory flights. Flyways may lie through the vast concrete canyons of gigantic cities where rest, food, and water are nonexistent, and ever-increasing skyscrapers and city lights present their peculiar hazards. Superhighways may be mistaken for rivers, with dire results. Airspace must be shared with giant planes. Lakes, gulfs, bays, even oceans must be crossed and vast mountains scaled. There is constant danger from storm. Pollution hangs like a pall over more and more of the countryside. Nesting habitats are fast changing or disappearing from field, marsh, and wood. Outboard motors poison lakes and streams. Forests provide welcome oases, but even these are shrinking under the onslaughts of civilization. Predators abound, the most insatiable of which is man, while sanctuary grows less and less. Small wonder, indeed, that more and more bird names are being added to the list of endangered species.

Yet migration continues. From south to north in spring, from north to south in fall, the wings press on — the tiny, fragile wings of the hummingbird, kinglet, and warbler — the mighty, pulsing wings of the eagle, swan, and heron — ceaselessly driving their owners onward toward their desired haven.

whistling swan

Nesting and breeding take place in the summer home, but the young are often only a few weeks old when instinct compels them to flock with their kind and set out for the wintering areas where they spend about three-quarters of each year. What teaches the young birds where to go, how to get there, how to survive en route? What instinct prompts many a returning adult in spring to find and nest in the identical branch of the identical tree or shrub in the identical yard, park, or roadside where he raised his family the previous year? How can the amazing feats of migration be accomplished?

Scientists have studied migration from every possible angle and have done countless experiments in their effort to unlock its secrets. Many books have been written about their endeavors, and interesting reading indeed they are; but migration to day remains what it always has been — an unsolved mystery.

The well-taught Christian may understand with his heart what he is unable to comprehend with his mind, thus, he may be in a better position than some to understand the mystery of migration.

God has put the homing instinct into the hearts of His birds, and they obey His sovereignty.

He has put the homing instinct into the hearts of His human children, too. Our home is God Himself, and we can never truly rest anywhere else.

God orders the migration of His feathered folk in such a way that neither natural nor man-made disasters can frustrate His purposes, but His will for His birds is accomplished.

Can we not trust Him to bring us safely to our eternal home when His time has come for us to enter His beloved presence?

Small Delights

Many are the small delights that await the observant bird watcher. For those who have eyes to see and ears to hear, lovely experiences abound on every hand. No one of them may be startlingly significant in itself, perhaps, but each is capable not only of flooding the day of its birth with beauty, but of creating memories that will bless with joy far into the future. Like the promises of God, many such happenings have burst in suddenly upon my most ordinary day, touching it with immortality.

My first sight of a pileated woodpecker, majestic ruler of the northern forest, was one such experience. What appeared to be a crow flying routinely across the river suddenly showed himself to be the mighty monarch to whose scarlet crown and ermine-tipped cloak I had long desired to pay homage. There he was, clinging to a tree before long, in all his regal splendor. And when, after several summers of admiring him, I one day watched him deliberately try to scare my aging Figaro by raising his crest and spreading his black and white wings at him, I marveled at his sly wit no less than at his awesome beauty.

A flicker who ate regularly at my suet feeder for two or three winters had an endearing habit. He would utter his low, plaintive cry until I would come to the window to watch him feed. No matter how cold might be the morning, or how hungry the bird, patiently he would call until I heard him and answered his summons. Only then would he feed upon the much-desired fatty food that he needed in winter when insects were few.

The sight of a scarlet tanager against a backdrop of deep forest is a sight both exciting and profoundly moving. During spring migration, most parks and ravines in our cities have their quota of these glorious, shy creatures; but only they who seek them diligently are likely to see them or hear the short, melodic phrases of their woodwindlike song. Yet one spring when illness confined me to the house during the whole of the migration season, a scarlet tanager visited me daily in my garden for almost a week. And a mocking bird, not actually unknown in Canada but so rare that many lifelong bird watchers have never seen one here, took up his abode along the ravine for a couple of weeks, pouring out his heart in glorious song as he sought a mate, often singing in my own shrubbery during that same shut-in spring. God's promises are ours to seek and find; but in times of special need, do they not sometimes find us out, unsought, to minister their grace to our spirits?

To hold a tiny wild creature in one's hand, however briefly, is to sense in a personal way something of the wonder of the universe. From time to time a bird will stun itself by flying against my picture window; some birds, like the chick-adee, are easily taught to eat from one's hand; and more than once I have rescued a bird from a cat, my own or another's. So I have held in my hand on occasion a fledgling bluebird, an infinitely tiny hummingbird, a shy veery, an olive-backed thrush, a tiny kinglet, a young song sparrow, orphaned orioles and flycatchers, and an assortment of house sparrows, robins, grackles, starlings, blue jays, crows, and blackbirds. To shelter that inert or shuddering little form, to stroke tenderly the tiny throat that can pulse with such sweet song, to watch the quivering eyelids open, then become steady, to look deeply into the suddenly aware, captive eyes, then a moment later to feel the small wings flex and whirr and see the little creature mount the air, wild and free once more, is to know something, however minute, of the creative joy of God.

The young of all species are appealing, but I

have found particular pleasure in viewing some juveniles who were so unlike their parents as to make their identification really difficult. Who would have thought that the large, grey, sober-eyed, crestless youngster sitting motionless on my mountain ash tree one whole morning last October was a cedar waxwing, his only likeness to his kind being the yellow band formed by the tips of his tail feathers? Or that the autumn immature of the red-headed woodpecker is garbed in two-toned grey, showing nothing of the scarlet, black, and white that makes his parents such a glory to behold, yet bearing about him just enough of their stance to enable one to make the connection between the two?

Only once have I seen a live woodcock. Her protective coloration provides her with such a perfect camouflage that most of my knowledge of woodcocks, bitterns, and other such hard-to-see birds has come to me through the amazing skill of naturalist photographers and their magnificent nature movies. This woodcock was sitting on her nest. Yet despite the fact that her position was pointed out to me by the keeper of the conservation area where I had taken a class of children for outdoor study, I stared at her for fully five minutes before I saw her, so much did she resemble the components of the heaped-up hillock of dead leaves and sticks which she had scraped together to make her untidy nest.

When finally I gazed into the calm brown eyes of the unmoving little woodcock who had seen me all too clearly during those long, tense minutes, threat to her nest that she knew me to be, I tiptoed away, awed, as from a holy place. It has not yet been my good fortune to hear what all true bird watchers long to hear — the mating song of this strange bird who sings for only a few brief minutes once a year on her nuptial flight, the rest of the time her voice being confined to a low, unmusical buzz.

To view the dazzling brilliance of a male cardinal against the winter's snow is no less thrilling than to hear him whistling his song of cheer from the top of a January-bare bough. To have a pair of cardinals as daily guests at one's feeder is to take much of the chill from the icy months of winter.

One winter a flock of about thirty redpolls joined the already resident group of slate-colored juncos that had come from the far Arctic tundra to winter along the edge of the ravine behind my home in Toronto. The juncos I have every winter; the redpolls came only that one year. What engaging little fellows they were with their sparrowlike backs topped by their bright red polls, the males

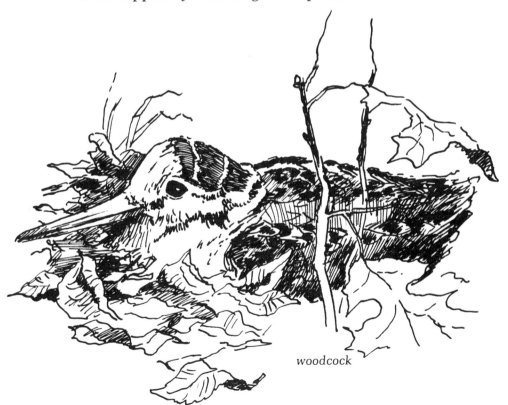

woodcock

with their bibs of red and a faint flushing of pink on greyish-white underparts! How I loved to see them circle down to alight at my feeder, bobbing up and down as they picked up seeds, chirping away cheerily no matter what the weather. To think that such lovely creatures actually surround the North Pole, coming a little distance south for only a few weeks in January and February; singing, breeding, and living out their little lives far from the sight of human eye, simply glorifying God and enjoying Him forever in the way He has ordained for them! Do I fulfill His purposes for me as truly?

Likeness

Within the embryo
  held fast in this small egg
lies all that goes to make the coming fledgling
    like to his kind

Here is the single touch of white
  at base of primary wing feathers
that sets the female black-throated blue warbler
  apart from all the hosts
of other olive-green yellow-washed
    female warblers

Here is the tree sparrow's lower mandible
  yellow but in part
its tiny tip
  matching the dusky upper,
here the pink bill
  of the field sparrow,
the yellow eye-stripe
  of the drab savannah,
the two white outer tail feathers
  that form a V
    in flying vesper sparrow,
the striped crown, yellow lores, and snowy bib
  that mark the whitethroat

Here is the flutelike song
  of hermit thrush
the wild, weird trumpeting
  of loon
the powerful, ringing cuk-cuk-cuk
  of pileated pecker
the bubbling crystal cascade
  of purple finch
the whispered lispings of kinglet
  and pine siskin

Here is the brilliant hue
  of blazing black-masked cardinal
of ruby-throated hummingbird
  of jet-winged scarlet tanager

of burnished breast of orange oriole
   of blue jay, grosbeak, goldfinch

Here are birds of forest or of field
   of mountain, tundra, ocean,
      lake, or plain
birds of towering treetops
   or of earth
cradled in grass or sticks
   or rocky ridge
swinging from branch
   or buried deep in tree trunk
each in the smallest detail
     like to his kind

And should it then seem strange
   that Christ in me —
His life made mine by faith
   wrought by His Spirit —
should perfect in my soul
   His holy image
till in that day
   when I shall see my Lord
despite my sin and weakness
   fear and failure
     I shall be found
       like Him?

Flight Patterns

sparrow hawk

The flight patterns of birds make a fascinating study, and many birds can be identified by their manner of flying alone. The whole woodpecker family, from the tiny downy to the giant pileated, has an undulating flight, dipping low in wide arcs then mounting again as they fly. It was this type of flying that made me take a second look at an apparent crow winging routinely across the river, only to discover, as he drew near enough for me to see clearly, that he was my first sighting of the rare pileated woodpecker. Several other birds undulate as they fly, but a great many of them do not; so undulation is a characteristic worth noting and investigating.

Many flight patterns, however, simply create visual delights for the beholder, displaying colors and markings not visible when the bird is at rest. The rufous-sided towhee and the rose-breasted grosbeak have exquisite white-on-black wing and tail markings that make a dazzling sight when the bird is flying. The meadowlark, the junco, and the vesper sparrow can be identified readily by the white V formed by their outer tail feathers when in flight. The mockingbird presents an exciting pattern of markings when airborne, as does the northern or the loggerhead shrike. Red-headed woodpeckers and pileated peckers display startlingly lovely markings in black, white, and scarlet. It is in flight that the rich saffron or crimson wing-and-tail-linings of the yellow- or red-shafted flicker are noon. Some of the most delicate markings of the tiny, multi-jeweled warbler family are visible only in flight, while hovering sparrow hawks are a shimmering glow of red and blue.

And across the most ordinary day such glories can flash forth — bright thoughts of God sent to remind His children of His sovereignty. Is it any wonder they leave reverence, awe, and praise in their wake?

Wood Warblers

It took me some years to build up enough familiarity with the wood warblers to be able to drink deeply of the joys their acquaintance offers, and there are many members of that lovely, elusive family that I do not yet know at all. But one Saturday afternoon in the peak of the migration period, and again on the Sunday, I sat in a tree-filled cemetery in midtown Toronto and watched a score of warblers at closest possible range to my heart's content. A wave of the little creatures had touched down to rest on their long flight from the tropics and the subtropics to the Canadian north woods, their breeding grounds, and, delayed by a cold front, had remained to await better traveling weather.

Black-throated blues and greens, both male and female, I had known before, though never had I been privileged to observe them so closely. But redstarts were new to me and were birds I had long wanted to see. Two pair of them fluttered about, seemingly oblivious of my presence or at least totally unconcerned about it. The males sang their faint, sweet, almost-whispered song; the females twittered softly in reply. Both spread their wings and tails constantly, the male displaying his characteristic orange markings, the female her yellow ones.

Chestnut-sided warblers, a male yellowthroat, a palm, a Kentucky, and a bay-breasted warbler flitted about in the sunshine, heedless of the cold May wind that saw me wrapped in my winter coat. Olive-backed and wood thrush in profusion foraged ceaselessly among the dried leaves of the underbrush. But the most thrilling of all my experiences that happy weekend, and the one remembered with the most excitement and pleasure, was watching the pair of magnolia warblers that moved gracefully in and out among the branches or

89

magnolia warbler

fed at my feet. Never have I seen anything more exquisite than those dainty yellow-breasted creatures with their glorious black-and-white-against-grey markings, the male with his black necklace flung in prodigal beauty against his golden throat. I watched in utter fascination, hour after hour, heedless of the biting wind, utterly transfixed by the revelation of my God and the wonder of His creation that came to me through His tiny warblers.

Wood warblers are found only in the Western Hemisphere; the blue-grey gnatcatcher and the ruby-crowned and the golden-crowned kinglet are the sole representatives in this hemisphere of the Old World warblers found across the ocean. Warblers are particularly difficult to study in the field for several reasons. They are very small, and they hop and flit about with incredible energy and speed in the leafy tops of the tall trees where they find most of their insect food. The adult males and females in breeding plumage are often colored quite differently from each other, and in the autumn they may be different again. Fledglings just out of the nest have one plumage, and by autumn the immatures have quite another. Though called warblers, they have no loud, sustained, sweet songs to attract attention and guide the watcher to their whereabouts, but rather an anomalous collection of lispings, hissings, creakings, and buzzes that seem to come from all directions at once and merely frustrate the listener. Yet partly because it is such a difficult thing to achieve and partly because of the exquisite beauty of the tiny birds when sought with patience and diligence and finally found, no bird sighting is more exciting, more humbling, or more rewarding than sightings of the wood warblers.

The hidden ways of God are something like His warblers — not always easily discerned. But the earnest seeker will find them to be ways of mercy and truth, righteousness and equity, joy, beauty, and peace.

Nuthatch

I had long enjoyed watching the white-breasted nuthatches that frequented my feeders and did their upside-down acrobatics on the tree trunks around the house and cottage. Their strange, urgent, nasal "yank, yank," sounding like anything but a bird, never failed to startle and amuse me, usually evoking delighted laughter. How ludicrously lovely that ridiculous little bird call is!

And what fun it is to watch the agile fellow, with his white face and breast, his blackish head and blue-grey back, and his unusually long wings and short tail, as he walks head downward around the tree trunks, working his way from the top to the base of the tree foraging for the grubs and other insects that are his food. Sunflower seeds on a feeder will assure the presence of this fascinating bird, who gets his name from his habit of inserting these and other nuts in crevices of bark, then hammering them with his bill till he cracks and eats them.

Never, however, had I seen his cousin the red-breasted nuthatch, whose white face is crossed by a black eye-line and whose breast is rusty rather than white. In southern Ontario these birds are usually seen only as migrants, generally living farther north. Though they are plentiful throughout the country, somehow I had never managed to see one.

One summer I drove for ten days across northern Michigan, crossing into Canada at Sault

Ste. Marie and returning home through northern Ontario, a bird watcher's paradise. I saw many beautiful birds, some of them for the first time; but never a red-breasted nuthatch did I see.

How well I remember drawing into my own driveway on the July afternoon when my journey ended! As I opened the car door, I heard a nuthatch calling from my spruce tree. Its voice was familiar — or was it? Wasn't there something slightly different about the intonation? Quickly I followed the sound with my eyes, and sure enough, there he was, inching downward headfirst — a red-breasted nuthatch! After all those miles of driving and watching, here was my long-sought bird welcoming me home.

How often do we seek God's presence, God's reality, God's guidance or blessing in far-off fields, in new experiences, in unusual happenings, only to find Him at last waiting for us in the common, humdrum round of the everyday!

nuthatch

Sights and Sounds

Some of my small delights have had to do with sudden sightings of birds in unexpected moments; others have come with the unexpected hearing of a burst of glorious song.

I remember coming upon a bittern once by a deserted, marshy stream, and recall startling a black-crowned night heron very early one spring morning in the ravine back of my home. There was the time that I came up from the dock at the river very late at night, and the beam of my flashlight caught in its glow a dear little wide-eyed sawhet owl sitting peacefully on my clothesline. I remember one bright day in October seeing a long-eared owl in a tree, looking down at me for all the world like Bugs Bunny up a tree. I recall the flight of pearly white gulls against a vicious black thundercloud as I rowed frantically for shelter during a summer storm at the river, and of a flock of water birds wheeling homewards against the backdrop of a glowing rose and amber sky. I see again the huge turkey vulture who considerately sat on a rock only a few feet from my window and groomed himself from stem to stern while I watched. I recall the swift, silent flight of an owl through the trees, the flashing drop of a kingfisher to seize a fish from the water far below. I relive my excitement at seeing my first wood thrush and watching a catbird in his leafy bower. I remember seeing an ovenbird sitting on a low bough, seemingly unaware of my presence. I shall never forget my first sighting and hearing an indigo bunting. And I remember the fiery darting of a tiny Blackburnian warbler and recall the time I heard him pour out his nuptial bliss in song from my neighbor's crab tree at five o'clock one sweet May morning.

The delight of hearing unexpected birdsong cannot be expressed in words, but it speaks to my spirit strongly of the things of God. To open my

sawhet owl

backdoor some frosty January morning and be greeted by the clear, sweet calling of the cardinal, the muttered, nasal "yak yak!" of the nuthatch, the low, excited squeal of the flicker and the shy, whistled "fee-bee!" of the chickadee's song moves me deeply. To hear the far, plaintive song of the white-throated sparrow and the fluted, crystal call of the thrush at the same door just before dawn in May will shake me to my heart's core. How many, many times my whole being has become silent before God — called into His presence in worship by the song of a bird!

The cheerful call of the eastern meadowlark is a welcome sound at any time, coming as it does long before most other migrants have returned. But once early on a cold May morning, I heard a meadowlark sing his marriage song from the tip of the highest spruce tree on the hill, filling the air with unbelievable beauty. On and on and on he sang; only my own eyes watching him convinced me that this glory on the air was indeed the work of my golden-breasted, black-laced friend. Similarly, on another occasion, a rufous-sided towhee sang his mating song in accents totally unlike his usual voice and exquisitely lovely. Likewise a goldfinch, departing from his usual song, sang a gloriously moving song of praise just at daylight through his August mating season. In each case I identified the singer by sight, not by sound, and have never found that music on records nor heard it repeated since.

A purple finch sang of love morning and night at the river one June, wakening me before five all through his nesting season. His song was his usual one, but more joyous, more ornate, and more richly embellished in honor of the occasion. Similarly with the rose-breasted grosbeak: his song, always lovely, is loveliest at nesting time. The housewren, whose liquid effervescent music is among the most melodious of our bird-songs at any time, outdoes herself at dawn in mating season. Never will I forget the first time I was awakened by a nesting wren singing early, early on a golden day in June! I had not known one small bird could contain so much beauty.

The kinglet is another small surprise. Next to the hummingbird, it is our tiniest bird, being smaller and shorter-tailed than the warbler family, though in other ways resembling them rather closely. What a surprise, then, to discover that that lengthy burst of joyous delight drifting down from the treetops on a crisp spring morning is the work of this feathered mite!

One August night I awakened at the river to hear the unmistakable call of the barred owl ringing through the woods nearby: "Hoo hoo . . . hoo hoo . . . . hoo hoo . . . hoo hoo — aw!" Sitting up in bed at 3 A.M., I hooted back, imitating his rhythmic pattern to the best of my ability. Evidently it suited him, for he replied, and we talked back and forth for twenty minutes before he considered the conversation closed. Similarly I have conversed with his kind from the boat when alone on the river at night, and I once held a discussion with a barred owl in an apple tree while lying in my own bed in Toronto. (Fortunately, perhaps, I live alone!) In any case, I find such experiences to be both beautiful and exciting!

A song of sudden delight ministered to my spirit one cold spring afternoon. It had rained hard for three days, yet I had been unable to bring myself to cancel a proposed field trip with my class of ten-year-olds. We went off down the slippery paths of the steep ravine to see what signs of spring were about.

We saw nothing. Not a bird, not a furred creature, scarcely a touch of green was visible. Then suddenly we heard the piping sweetness of a singing song sparrow. Never have I heard such a song of utter ecstasy! We could not see him — we never did sight him — but we stood there in the sodden path, all thirty-five of us, in total silence; the rushing of a small spring freshet behind us, the glory of the sparrow's song all about us. He sang for fully five minutes. We were content to return home then, refreshed and rejoicing in heart, satisfied that spring had, indeed, come to our city.

So God sends us His small delights to cheer us on our homeward way!

High Fliers

I had never paid particular attention to the common crow until I moved to a house high on a hill which overlooked a deep, grassy ravine, giving me an unbroken view of the sky for more than half a mile. Great winds would come sweeping up the valley, and on windy days only crows and an occasional hawk would inhabit the broad expanse I enjoyed from my picture window.

There they would soar, high above the earth, reveling in the same winds that kept smaller birds close to the shrubbery, the grass, or a sheltering stand of wood. What a sight it was to see them floating on the air currents, their black scarcely moving wings gleaming strangely white in the brilliant sunshine, wing tips extended like the fingers on a hand, alternately gliding, drifting, dropping, then mounting the turbulent air at will!

It has not yet been my good fortune to watch eagles fly, but gradually my experience of birds has broadened to include many kinds of hawks and falcons, vultures, ospreys and other soaring water birds, all of which ride thermal currents in similar fashion. But it was the lowly crow who first showed me the grace and beauty of the high fliers, and I shall always be grateful to him, thief and robber that I know him to be!

All of these birds are totally at home in what is to other birds a hostile environment. They delight in high winds and use them to attain their own ends, for they are able to ride the same currents that would drive other creatures to their destruction.

So it may be with us. God wants His children to learn to use the winds of adversity which He allows to beat upon them, not to be defeated and

98

osprey

impoverished by them. God Himself rides the wings of the storm, using stormy winds to fulfill His Word. Need we fear to learn to mount the thermal currents of our lives and ride them in company with our sovereign God?

Flight Plan

O flashing wings
  soaring on high
so powerfully
  gracefully
    effortlessly

So freely
  cleaving the shining skies
    mounting the morning breezes
      riding the raging winds

      drifting above the meadow
        hovering over the valley
          gliding across green waters

Watching you
  how my earthbound spirit
longs to cast off the fetters
    of mortality
        longs to be free!

But hush, my soul!

    One golden moment
  sudden, unlooked-for, swift
        as twinkling eye

the silver trump shall sound
  and I be clothed
    with immortality

Set free from sin
  and earth's imprisoning bonds

I shall arise

  swifter than bird
    fairer than dawning day
      stronger than eagles' wings

I shall arise
  to meet my Lord!

Sheltering Wings

I had been watching the nest from the day it was completed, a rough, untidy-looking mixture of twigs and grasses lined with soft rootlets and plant fibers. It was perched rakishly in the crotch of a slim branch of a young birch tree overhanging the waters of the river.

The mother kingbird was sitting on four eggs, assisted by her mate who hovered about protectively. Her black head with its pearly white throat protruded from one side of the nest, black eyes keenly alert; her black tail, edged with its distinctive band of white, showed beyond the other side. She did not look particularly comfortable, but there she would sit, most of the time almost motionless, during the twelve or thirteen days required to incubate her eggs; and she would remain there for as long afterwards as the nestlings needed her care.

Cradling her eggs beneath her, she warmed them with her soft, white breast. Most female birds, and some males, have brood patches for the incubation of their eggs and care of their young. Birds' feathers do not grow continuously over their bodies, but rather grow in tracts and spread out to cover the bare areas. During nesting season the natural bare areas in the breast become highly vascularized, and when the feathers are parted form a brood patch capable of transmitting direct body heat to the eggs or nestlings.

Daily I would paddle over to visit the nest. Once while I was moored nearby, a sudden squall blew up. Curious to see how the kingbird would fare in the lashing wind and driving rain of a summer thunderstorm, I decided to risk the elements myself and remain there.

The branches were thrashing about wildly, tossing the nest severely. If it had broken, its precious burden would have crashed to the swirling waters below. But mother kingbird had built well; her nest held.

Why did it not fill with water and drown the babies, I wondered, noting how rapidly the water was rising in my boat. It was then that I saw why the nest needed no bailing. The mother bird had spread her wings in such a manner that her body formed a perfect watershed for her nest as she crouched over it, her thick, oily wing-feathers shedding the water like a peaked roof, little streams of water pouring off the edges all the way around. Despite the tossing of the wind and the driving rain, her little family was warm, safe, and dry in their nest, protected by the discomfort of her own body.

Sometimes a late spring storm will leave early-nesting birds sitting on their nests in the icy cold, covered with snow or sleet, but sheltering their young. And following forest fires, it is said, live fledglings have been found huddled beneath the outstretched wings and the dead bodies of their mothers. I read recently of a bird-loving motorist who stopped his car one night to remove a dead quail from the center of the road, only to discover that the little creature was very much alive, sheltering four tiny chicks beneath her outstretched wings. They had been unable to join the rest of the flock at the edge of the road at the car's approach, so she had tried the only way she knew to save them — by covering them with her sheltering wings.

One extremely hot day I visited the kingbird's nest about noon to find that it was lying in the full blaze of a burning sun. Once again mother kingbird had spread her wings, this time to shelter her nestlings from the heat. There she crouched in the almost intolerable midday heat, her bill agape, her body heaving as she panted breathlessly, the only means she had of cooling herself. But inside the nest, sheltered by the mother's wings, all was cool and dark, and the little ones slept peacefully.

On many occasions I have watched parent birds teach their young to fly. Here the wings are used in a different manner, varying from species to species, but all variations of behavior serving the same purpose — to protect the fledglings from falling should fear or ineptitude render their own little wings ineffective.

Sometimes individually, sometimes shepherding the flock all at one time, the parent birds will encourage the fledglings to leave their nest or their safe perch. Then when the young are airborne, the parent birds will zoom in below them, wings spread wide, to catch and support them should they falter or fall. Since I witness such wonders mainly at the river, the first flying lessons are usually carried on over the water where no aid would be available should the youngster fall. Yet in over thirty years of watching first flights here, I have never seen a nestling plunge to his death yet — always there were welcoming wings outstretched to receive him.

The red-tailed hawk launches his family here each July. High, high in the air above this rocky Canadian shield, so high that even the parent birds appear as tiny dots in the blue and only their wild, high-pitched screams arouse my attention, they fling their precious young into the abyss below, guiding them and sheltering them from harm with their own strong bodies and powerful wings. How true, how strong are their sheltering wings!

It does not seem strange to me that the God who made the wings of His wild things, who planted deep in their beings the instinct to use them in the nurture and preservation of their young, should speak in similar imagery of His own care of His human children.

kingbird

"I bore you on eagles' wings, and brought you unto myself," He tells us (Exod. 19:4). "As an eagle stirreth up her nest, fluttereth over her young, spreadeth abroad her wings, taketh them, beareth them on her wings: so the Lord alone did lead him" (Deut. 32:11). "He shall cover thee with his feathers, and under his wings shalt thou trust" (Ps. 91:4). Such are His assurances and promises to us.

The sheltering wings of God are wide and strong. Shall we not look up to Him in confidence and pray, "Hide me under the shadow of thy wings" (Ps. 17:8)? And soon we shall exclaim with the psalmist, "Because thou hast been my help, therefore in the shadow of thy wings will I rejoice" (Ps. 63:7).

Binoculars

It was not until I looked at an oriole through a good pair of binoculars that I really became a serious bird watcher.

How I allowed so many years to slip away before I awakened to the wonders of bird watching, I am at a loss to explain. For many years I had summered at my riverside home, intensely aware of the beauties around me, one with nature and enjoying it, as I thought, to the full. Birds were a part of that beauty, of course; I exulted to their wheeling wings against the sky or water, their dawn chorus and evening song recitals. But I saw them only with the naked eye; my near-sightedness and their inherent quickness of motion combined to keep me from really seeing anything much smaller than gulls, terns, loons, ducks, herons, or an occasional kingfisher, and even these I seldom saw in detail. I had no idea of the infinite number and variety and the exquisite beauty of the birds that frequent our great outdoors.

Then came the day when a friend handed me a pair of binoculars, pointed to a bright spot high in a tree, and said, "Look at that!" I looked — and what I saw changed the whole pattern of my life. From that moment I became an avid bird watcher, and words are powerless to express the new dimensions of joy that have opened before me as a result.

Through binoculars I can really see a bird. His size, his shape, his coloring, the fine points of his markings, all can be observed in close detail. The bird himself can be studied — his feeding, mating, and nesting habits; his manner of grooming himself, of singing; his flight patterns; his behavior and intelligence; his life as a member of a complex social order; his whole amazing personality is revealed to me through the medium of my glasses.

How do binoculars do this? Their lenses are made to bring to the eye more light than it can gather by itself; hence they illuminate the birds. They have the capacity of bringing distant objects much closer to the observer and of magnifying them to several times their real size. Thus I can see in a new way, and study with my own eyes, the wonders of bird life.

Binoculars also make the field guide come alive to the bird watcher. The beautifully painted pictures in the book are only pictures until the power of the binoculars focuses on the bird itself, causing it to leap into life for the beholder. The wonders depicted in the book only become real in actual experience through the use of binoculars.

I have discovered that a rare fellowship exists among persons who belong to the fraternity of the field glass. Two strangers carrying binoculars will chance to meet in a park, at the shore, or along a dusty roadside, and almost immediately they are friends, sharing their experiences in bird-watching.

Does not all of this find a ready parallel in the Christian life? The Scriptures, our spiritual guide, are but printed pages until God's Holy Spirit sheds His light upon them, bringing the words to life and applying their truths to our hearts. As the binoculars, to be useful to us, must focus upon an object outside themselves and illumine and magnify it, so the Spirit does not speak of Himself, but shows us the beauties of Jesus Christ and glorifies Him.

Just as it takes a little time for a new bird watcher to learn to derive maximum pleasure and use from his binoculars, so a deep knowledge of the Savior is not acquired in a day. As we learn to obey the laws of optics with regard to our glasses, we find that they reveal more and more hidden wonders to our sight. And so in obedience to the laws of the Spirit, we learn more and more of the beauties of the One on whom all our soul's vision is centered.

The bird watcher soon will find that he must stand in the right relationship to the light if he wishes to see birds. The light must shine on the bird, not in the viewer's eyes. If he tries to look at a bird against the light, all color is lost and all birds appear black. Need more be said?

It is exciting when sitting scanning the heavens with binoculars to see appear in the lenses birds which one had been quite unable to discern with the naked eye. In a seemingly empty heaven, there are the birds — like the presence of God, which is ours whether we are aware of it or not. The Spirit can bring it into focus for us and make it real in our experience.

As our understanding of the things of God increases, so does our joy; a delight beyond telling fills our days as our whole being is transformed by the living Word of God made real in our lives by His Spirit. And we experience a richness of fellowship we never knew could exist as we recognize His life in others and rejoice together in the oneness and riches we share in our Savior, Jesus Christ.

Awareness

I had not been seriously interested in birds for very long before I began to be aware that subtle changes were taking place deep within me.

When I wakened early, instead of turning over and going back to sleep, I found myself wanting to get up to listen to the growing chorus of bird-song that began before dawn with a few isolated pipings and swelled to a glorious crescendo of morning praise. Somehow sleep seemed less important to me now than bird-watching, and to this day I feel that I have my most intimate and exciting adventures with birds and hear their loveliest and most abandoned singing in the hours of the early morning. I think that bird watchers in general will agree with this; there is a special glory to morning music that seems never quite recaptured later in the day.

I found that I carried my binoculars and field guide about with me most of the time, even when out on commonplace errands or routine travel. Birds are vagrant and unpredictable creatures and are apt to turn up almost anywhere at the most unlooked-for times, as when a gorgeous cock pheasant solemnly skimmed a few inches above the hood of my car and crossed four lanes of rush-hour traffic on Toronto's main thoroughfare as I drove to school one morning. The glasses were used unexpectedly on many occasions.

Odd minutes in subways or buses were no longer wasted, but whiled away happily in studying my field guide, until gradually sizes, shapes, colors, markings, and flight patterns, at first so bewildering, began to become distinguishable to me. That well-known bugbear of the teaching profession, yard duty, became more tolerable as I realized suddenly that the same circling glances that swept the playground while supervising children could also sweep the skies; and though there was no time to use binoculars in this instance, duty days became less onerous as I learned to identify more completely with the clouds, the winds, the sun, rain, or snow, and to enjoy whatever birds might be about, as well as watching my children.

My perception heightened, both visually and aurally, to quite a surprising degree. I have worn glasses from early childhood and am very near-sighted; this is probably one reason why I remained largely unaware of birds for as many years as I did. Yet once aroused, I was amazed at what I began to be able to see, even when not using my binoculars. I developed a peripheral vision I had never known before; eventually I could detect a bird flying almost behind me. Stirring leaves or grasses, a bending reed, a subtle movement in a well-screened, leafy bough — those minute signs of the presence of hidden birds — gradually became visible to me, then began to lead to happy sightings.

Even more delightful were the tiny sounds I had never noticed before but now began to hear: a soft sibilance overhead, that almost inaudible whisper by means of which many birds announce their presence while purposely remaining totally concealed; the snapping of a single twig; the rustle of a blade of grass or of one flower; the folding of a wing; the delicate footfall of a silently alighting bird on a branch, a tree trunk, or the grass — these became sounds that I could hear and interpret and use to discover the nearness of a bird. And I learned to listen to the birds themselves — to their calls, their alarm notes, their conversational tones, their songs, even their lullabies, until I began to be able to distinguish many of them solely by sound.

I had never found spending time alone to be a tedious thing, but now such time became newly precious. While the presence of an experienced

ring-necked pheasant

bird-watching friend can be very enjoyable, bird-watching is essentially an individual thing and is probably best carried out in solitude. With glasses and guide book at hand, hours sped by like minutes, every moment crammed with delight as I communed in a new way with the wonders around me — alone, yet never lonely.

In fact, all of nature soon took on added dimensions. Forests, woods, brushlands, fields, meadows, marshlands, waters, hills, valleys, tablelands, plant life of every description — all became things to be observed, noted, and studied. For these things are the essence of environment and determine habitat, and, when wisely interpreted, tell what varieties of wildlife one may expect to find in any particular situation.

Are not such experiences but a faint reflection of the riches of the new life God gives us in Jesus Christ? As Christ becomes Lord in our lives, we experience the expulsive power of a new affection, transforming our thoughts and desires, realigning our priorities, modifying our interests and pursuits. The morning hour with Him comes to be jealously guarded. The Guide Book is ever present, and with it the binoculars — the Holy Spirit who reveals the things of Christ to us. A new urgency fills our days; a new Companionship pervades every area of our life.

> Heaven above is softer blue,
>   Earth around is sweeter green;
> Something lives in every hue
>   Christless eyes have never seen.

Birds with gladder songs o'erflow,
   Flowers with deeper beauties shine,
Since I know, as now I know,
   I am His, and He is mine.

            — Rev. Wade Robinson

The deepening of awareness, the heightening of perception, the sharpening of the sensibilities, the growing sense of wonder, joy, and awe as we contemplate God and His greatness displayed in whatever manner — these are God's gifts in Jesus Christ to all His children. And who should know and love God's world more than we who know Him redemptively and re-creatively in Christ?

Never Too Late

It is never too late in life to become a bird watcher. Wonderful as it must be to grow up in full awareness and knowledge of nature's wonders, lack of such opportunity need not deter anyone who wishes to join the ranks of those who observe and learn and delight in God's creative handiwork.

I know. For despite the fact that I have now retired after thirty-eight years of teaching children, it is only within the last five years that birds have been a significant part of my life. Almost all the experiences chronicled here, and all observations made and knowledge gained, have taken place within those years, and for four of them I was still in the classroom, with limited time to spend out-doors.

That I am unable now to walk any distance or to stand for any length of time, even to carry my binoculars around my neck for very long, while creating certain problems, does not preclude my taking part in outdoor birding activities, even if on a somewhat reduced scale. I carry a light aluminum stool on my walks and sit every avail-able minute, finding that it is much easier to sight from a sitting than a standing position even if it were not a physical necessity. I use the car when I can, idling along back roads. I watch from a recum-bent position on the floor of a small aluminum boat — surely the most practical and comfortable way of using binoculars! Sometimes I watch water birds while floating on my back in the warm waters of the river, scanning the skies and letting wind and wave carry me where they will — although I do not take my glasses on this kind of jaunt! I lure birds to the house or cottage by providing a great number and variety of feeders, mostly homemade and of my own invention. I do most of my work sitting by wide windows or outside if at all possible, where the faintest sound or slightest flick of a wing is immediately audible and visible.

All in all, I manage to see and hear quite a number of birds.

Nature films, Audubon societies, and a splendid array of library books on ornithology are available to all, and I have derived a great deal of information and pleasure from such things. And of course I am long since a member of my local fellowship of bird watchers.

I regret the lost years, of course — years when I could tramp for miles in any weather and stand gazing upwards for hours, years when I had the keen eyes and ears and retentive memory of youth — bifocals are no asset, I must admit. I regret particularly the number of summers I spent at the river when, while reveling in the outdoor life I lived there and enjoying it as I thought to the full, somehow I managed to miss the wonders of the proliferation of bird life around me, considering it merely a part of nature's background, not the integral, revitalizing, joyous thing that it is in itself. Those opportunities are gone and will not come again. The river has built up rapidly these past fifteen years, and wildlife of all kinds is retreating. However, there is no point in regret; there is still today and, in the providence of God, tomorrow and the day after that. Starting from where one is today, it is never too late to become a bird watcher and to enter into the joys of the bird-watching fellowship.

It is never too late, either, to make a Christian commitment, to become a member of that greatest fellowship on earth — the body of believers by faith in the Savior, the Lord Jesus Christ.

Sovereign God, He became man for us, lived in our world, knew our joys and sorrows, died our death that we might be freed from the penalty of our sin. Death could not hold Him, Prince of Life that He is; He arose in triumph over sin and death and lives today — lives forever in the power of His endless life and in the hearts and lives of those who own Him as Savior and Lord.

The day has not yet come when He will return to this earth as Lord and King to receive from all humanity the homage due to His name, but come it will; then every knee will bow before Him, every tongue confess Him Lord. Meanwhile, He calls out His children, His Church and Bride, one by one; and whoever hears His voice may come and take of the Water of Life freely, drinking deeply and yet more deeply of His life on earth and finally sharing in His glory forever in His Heaven.

It may be that you have lived in His world oblivious to the spiritual wonders about you, as I did for so many years as far as birds were concerned. You may have lived your life against a background of Christianity without ever realizing its significance for you personally, or the joys that could be yours. If this should be your moment of truth concerning commitment to Jesus Christ, act now. Start where you are today and call upon His name as Savior and Lord. Young or old, rich or poor, sick or well, it makes no difference — it is never too late to become a Christian!

Pond Lily

Heart of cleft gold
   quivering with beauty,
fragrant
   with breath of skies,
white
   with the blinding purity of holiness,
You are found among us,
   not afar,
breasting the murky waters
   of our humanity;
a tender plant
   rooted in muck,
yet diffusing
   to those who stoop to pluck you
      the Life of Heaven.